MW00778198

MYTHS AND MYSTERIES

OF

MISSOURI

TRUE STORIES
OF THE UNSOLVED AND UNEXPLAINED

JOSHUA YOUNG

Guilford, Connecticut
Helena, Montana
An imprint of Rowman & Littlefield

An imprint of Rowman & Littlefield

Distributed by NATIONAL BOOK NETWORK

British Library Cataloguing-in-Publication Information available

Library of Congress Cataloging-in-Publication Data available

ISBN 978-0-7627-7226-1 (paperback)

∞™ The paper used in this publication meets the minimum requirements of American National Standard for Information Sciences—Permanence of Paper for Printed Library Materials, ANSI/NISO Z39.48-1992.

CONTENTS

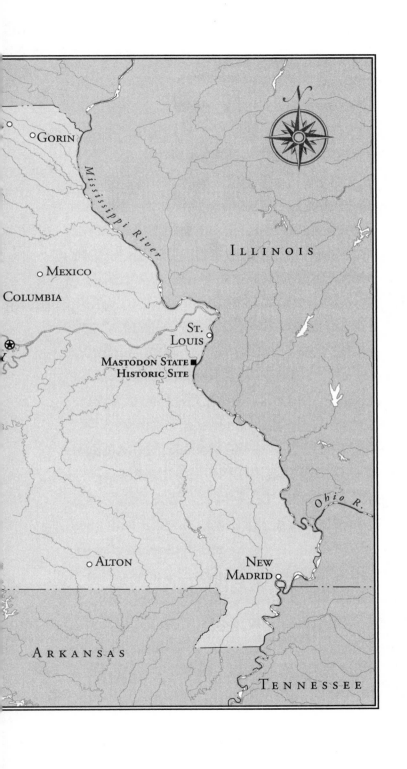

INTRODUCTION

"I'm from Missouri; you've got to show me."

Well, okay, I'm not from Missouri, but I live here now, and the same could have been said by Willard Duncan Vandiver, the congressman who uttered this famous quotation during a legislative debate in 1899.

The full quote that gave Missouri her nickname as "The Show Me State" goes, "I come from a country that raises corn and cotton, cockleburs and Democrats, and frothy eloquence neither convinces nor satisfies me. I'm from Missouri, and you have got to show me."

Vandiver was actually born in Virginia, moving to Missouri with his parents three years later in 1857, but by the time he uttered his famous remark, the place where he had been born had become West Virginia. Explaining all that would have diminished his rhetorical flair, so you can see why he made it shorter and sweet. Back then, when you made a speech in Congress, you were actually talking to a quorum of your colleagues, not just a CNN crew.

I'm from Rhode Island and I traveled around quite a bit, living in several states before I settled here in Missouri more than thirty years ago. Before I lived here, I was one of those kids who thought Missouri was pretty boring when viewed from the backseat of my parents' car—just a big croquet wicket to drive by in St. Louis, some woods, a bunch of corn and soybeans, a few Burma Shave signs, and lots of barns painted to advertise Meramec Caverns with its Jesse James hideout.

Once I settled here, I discovered Missouri was one of the best-kept secrets in the United States. I was first drawn to the recreational opportunities: broad expanses of unbroken forests, large lakes, magnificent rivers, fascinating caves, plus varied hiking and biking trails. Next I came to appreciate the cities, topped by the distinct personalities of Kansas City and St. Louis, but with nice little surprises like Columbia, Springfield, and Joplin. Branson, with its screaming billboards, tourists on pilgrimage, and acres of theater seats, is in a category all by itself. At heart I am a small-town guy, so I love to find a colorful farmers' market on a town square, a good local restaurant, or a forty-mile-long yard sale.

Missouri is filled with people who live here because they love it. Native Missourians leave home to see the world and discover the world is not so much better than what they had at home. Folks from elsewhere discover Missouri and wonder why people who were born here ever wanted to go anyplace else. People from the East and West Coasts hesitate to buy real estate in Missouri, because at these prices, with such low taxes, they figure something has got to be wrong with the house.

But Missouri does not reveal her secrets easily. For one thing plenty of our real estate is below the surface. This is a cave state and a mining state. We have what is said to be the world's largest underground lake, formed by a mine so vast mules spent their entire lives down there, toiling underground. With all these caves and tunnels, you will not be surprised to hear we have plenty of treasure and loot, like the Lost Silver Mine of the Ozarks and a rumored shipment of hidden Confederate gold in the Lost Civil War Cave.

Politically Missouri mirrors the divisions within our country, with a difficult Civil War past that divided neighbors, and modern-day issues that keep us flickering back and forth between red and blue. We are the only state that ever elected a dead guy to the US Senate. That year you could have said Missouri's motto was "Better dead than red."

Missouri is a stepping-off place, as symbolized by the Gateway Arch in St. Louis. This was where Lewis and Clark set off on their Corps of Discovery Expedition; where the Santa Fe and Oregon Trails began; and where Pony Express riders set off at a gallop across the West. Missouri also sent legendary explorers and reckless adventurers to the East, with feats like Charles Lindbergh's famous flight across the Atlantic in the *Spirit of St. Louis,* and the lesser-known, but even more harrowing, first ever attempted airmail flight. (Check it out; those airmail balloonists back in the day were like an out-of-control reality show.)

Plenty of locals have driven over to witness the Spooklight, south of Joplin, but we don't much care if you believe our stories about it or not. Whereas other states would try to make a tourist attraction out of something so mysterious and unusual, we make parking difficult and give misleading directions that send you over to Oklahoma, if you're not from around these parts.

Some people would rather not tell you quiet Missouri experienced at least three of the largest earthquakes in the recorded history of the world, just a couple hundred years ago, because many scientists say some such event could easily happen again. (Only, whenever next time is, the damage will be much, much worse.) Instead we suggest you put on your happy face and drive on over to Branson or Joplin, and just ignore the evidence of where those recent record tornadoes tore through. Don't be afraid to come and visit. Remember: Most accidents happen in your home.

Missourians put a different spin on our legendary brazen crimes and gruesome murders. Jesse James is celebrated here like a Robin Hood hero; so too are Bonnie and Clyde, the stop-and-rob couple who rampaged here from Texas. The shocking broad daylight "Kansas City Massacre" of three police officers, an FBI agent, and their criminal witness at Union Station in 1933 is somewhat proudly mentioned as the justification for why FBI agents can now carry guns. Missouri is where you heard about the town bully who was gunned down in front of a crowd of townspeople who all just happened to be looking the other way at the time, and where the Three Springfield Women simply vanished from a quiet neighborhood without any sign of a struggle or even leaving a trace.

But don't worry about Missouri crime. Author Daniel Woodrell, who wrote the chilling novel *Winter's Bone,* set here in Missouri, comfortingly reminds us that most of those awful crimes in the news are committed by people who know each other. Stick with strangers, but avoid your family and friends; that way, statistically speaking, you'll probably be all right.

Missouri has not bragged enough about some of her legendary heroes, and as a result, today a few of them are largely unknown and way underappreciated. Tom Bass worked miracles with horses, in ways people who have not witnessed a horse whisperer still think are impossible. In the process, rising out of slavery, Tom Bass changed the way ordinary horses would be treated forever, and made significant progress to elevate his race. He was the Jackie Robinson of his sport; he was the George Washington Carver of his profession.

The Missouri Giantess, Ella Ewing, grew taller than any woman ever known, rising above widespread ignorance and superstition to transform herself from a ridiculed "freak" into a wealthy, gracious lady. The path she walked was epic, when measured alongside how we treat anyone who is "different" today.

If you are looking for animal monsters, check out Missouri mastodons, although, on closer examination, you will see they were more often victims than killers. Dude, you think you're livin' Paleo? Try killing a six-ton animal with tools you made with your bare hands next time you get hungry.

When you think of giant celebrities, you can't get any bigger or more recognizable than the Beatles, but they successfully hid here in Missouri for a little summer vacation they would remember for the rest of their lives. It was maybe one of the last times the legendary musicians would be treated just like regular blokes. "You may be famous someplace else, but breakfast ain't quite ready, so grab that broom and sweep off the front porch, wouldja, Honey?"

There is so much that is mythical and mysterious and flat out amazing about Missouri I can't begin to tell it all. Some of this is what I call "Woo-woo," and some of it is just plain "Wow." There are things I can tell you, you would not believe. Now imagine yourself flying through the Gateway Arch . . . Welcome to Missouri!

CHAPTER 1

Jim the Wonder Dog

Was Jim the Wonder Dog really an "old soul" revisiting the world in the form of a not-show-quality bird dog, or an amazing con, pulled off without any apparent purpose of financial gain? Could there have been another ulterior motive to explain his mysterious feats and extraordinary knowledge? If he was the product of an elaborate hoax, how could his master have consistently hoodwinked experts and seasoned skeptics, like professors of psychology, professors of veterinary medicine, and a joint session of the Missouri State Legislature? Could a dog really do everything newspaper reporters witnessed and initial disbelievers saw and talked about for the rest of their lives? We may never know.

I would be less inclined to believe the stories about Jim the Wonder Dog if I did not have direct knowledge of another remarkable canine. That seemingly wise, perhaps psychic, but beyond a doubt extraordinarily intelligent dog lived decades after the world-famous Jim the Wonder Dog, and over 1,000 miles away, in my hometown of East Greenwich, Rhode Island. (You can even find articles about this famous dog from my childhood on the Internet.)

My father was a family physician, well steeped in science as an undergraduate before attending Harvard Medical School. By nature he was open-minded, yet skeptical, and highly observant because of his medical training. Among his patients when I was growing up were George and Marion Wood, whose dog, Chris, attained fame with appearances on television's *I've Got a Secret* and *The Gary Moore Show*. Chris was also studied by a Duke University professor who described him in the respected *Journal of Parapsychology*.

Back when doctors making house calls were not rarer than dogs with psychic powers, my dad often attended the Woods in their home. As part of the routine greeting, visitors would encounter Chris and bear witness to some small act of apparent canine clairvoyance.

Mr. Wood, an engineer by profession, found he enjoyed training his various pets at home. This went beyond, "Sit!" and "Roll over!" He made a hobby of trying to teach his dogs to count out numbers with their paws and indicate letters of the alphabet with a similar system he devised. Mr. Wood had even tried to teach tricks to his parakeet, but he was just glad when he could get that bird to return to its cage. He hadn't gotten very far with any of his experiments in pet training when one day, while he was trying to teach his favorite dog to count, his wife asked Chris, a recently adopted stray, if he could count to ten. Chris promptly pawed her arm ten times, as her husband was trying to teach their other dog to do. On that day George Wood shifted his entire focus to Chris.

Some doubters dismissed Chris's demonstrated ability to add, spell, predict winning race horses, and report sports scores from the radio as nothing more than "the Clever Hans Phenomenon," whereby a trainer gives unconscious clues to an animal. But all the kids (and most of the adults) in the neighborhood believed George Wood to be entirely sincere when he said he employed no trickery when he demonstrated the extraordinary abilities of his little beagle mutt Chris. When Chris spelled out his opinion of cats (DUMB) and the reason for his extraordinary abilities (SMARTDOG), for Duke University researchers, my father said the dog was demonstrating a sense of humor he never saw George Wood muster.

Unlike the questionable ancestry of my hometown hero Chris Wood, Jim the Wonder Dog had proud parentage leading back through generations of Llewellin setters. His kin were high-dollar bird dogs. Born March 10, 1925, as part of a large litter in Louisiana, Jim was a funny-looking runt. Fate matched him with an initially unenthusiastic owner from Missouri named Sam VanArsdale.

Jim's future man pal Sam supposedly said, "That's the ugliest dog I've ever seen," and nobody seemed to think he was just trying to get the asking price down. Jim truly was a homely ambassador for his breed. Under different circumstances back then a seemingly listless, runty pup might have been shot or drowned. One story has it VanArsdale got Jim for one-fifth the going price for a good

Jim The Wonder Dog

Lovers of the breed say Jim was a homely Lewellin setter.

hunting dog, and kept him as a joke among hunting buddies, or at the very least an attempt to prove them wrong for spite.

Jim's promise looked none too good when Sam began trying to train him with his other bird dogs back home in Missouri. The young pup seemed oblivious to any commands given, preferring instead to merely watch from the shade while the older dogs carried out their commands with mixed success. But the first time VanArsdale took Jim out alone to hunt, without hesitation the dog located a covey of quail, went on perfect point, and when told to fetch, immediately retrieved the first bird the hunter shot.

VanArsdale was an avid hunter who often took his dogs beyond Missouri on hunts with other sportsmen. Beginning to believe he might have an outright fine hunting dog in Jim, Van Arsdale kept count of the birds the still young setter had helped him take, and by the time he was full grown the dog had been written up in more than one hunting magazine as a setter of some promise. *Outdoor Life* called him "The Hunting Dog of the Century." Now hunters are generally fond and proud of their best dogs, but there is no indication VanArsdale thought initially he had anything better than an outstanding, if ugly, retriever, now always eager to hunt.

When Jim was three, VanArsdale took him alone on a particularly tiring hunt one very hot day. Needing to rest himself, the hunter spoke conversationally to his dog, saying, "Jim, let's go rest a bit under a hickory tree for a while." Jim obediently trotted over to a hickory and sat down.

Amused by the seeming coincidence, the master commanded, "Well, if you're so smart, why don't you show me a walnut tree?" The obedient Jim promptly did. Accounts vary as to what species of trees Jim identified that particular day, but all agree that in no time at all Jim showed himself adept at identifying a pretty wide assortment of trees (plus a can and a stump), which is something not a lot of humans can do with both hands, a magnifying glass, and a field guide.

Not long after, a pregnant stray cat showed up at the hotel VanArsdale owned in Sedalia. For fun Sam wrote "male" on five slips of paper and "female" on another five; he then placed all the choices in front of Jim, asking him to predict the litter. This Jim did correctly, selecting two males and three females by pawing at the slips of paper. When word of that feat got around, VanArsdale was asked to have Jim predict the sex of several unborn human babies, which he performed correctly on at least six separate occasions. At some point these requests seem to have unnerved the generally obliging innkeeper, because he thereafter made it a rule to refuse such requests as something he did not believe God intended.

VanArsdale said he never sought to profit from his canine friend, so when Jim began successfully picking race horses, there is no record of Sam betting on the outcomes. But one evening, when a group of VanArsdale's friends were sitting around talking about the Kentucky Derby, they asked if Jim could pick the winner. VanArsdale wrote the name of each horse in the race on separate slips of paper and sealed each in an envelope. He then handed the envelopes out to his friends, so no one knew which horse's name he held. Jim made a selection and that envelope, still sealed, was placed in a safe until after the race. When the Derby had been run and the envelope was opened, it contained the name of the winning horse. In similar fashion Jim correctly picked the names of the next six Kentucky Derby winners.

A widely publicized test of Jim's amazing abilities was held at Missouri University in Columbia, where Paramount studios filmed the proceedings. Faculty members from several institutions across Missouri were invited to participate. First professors from the School of Veterinary Medicine and the Agriculture

Department examined Jim and stated they found nothing remarkable. He seemed to be just an ordinary dog.

Jim was then asked to find a Professor Dickinson, which he did in no time. Invited to ask questions of Jim in a setting outdoors on campus, the assembled group of students and faculty gamely tried to stump the pooch. One asked in Italian for Jim to find an elm tree, which he proved he could do. Next he was asked in French to locate a car with a particular license number. Again Jim was correct. Jim found a girl in a blue dress when asked to do so in German, and likewise a man with a black moustache, when so requested in Spanish. It has been pointed out by many who knew him that VanArsdale spoke nothing but English, so could give his dog no clues. After the lengthy demonstration, the gathered animal experts, as well as psychologists from Missouri University and Washington University in St. Louis, declared through their spokesman, Dr. A. J. Durant, the dog known as Jim "possessed an occult power that might never come again to a dog in many generations." In 1933 the Missouri legislature convened in joint session to see a demonstration by Jim. On that occasion it was recorded he found people by name (whom VanArsdale did not know) and correctly picked people by descriptions of their complexions and the colors of their clothes. Many of those instructions were given to Jim in Morse code, which VanArsdale had never learned. (And experts will tell you most dogs are apparently color-blind.) In response to a final command given to the setter, again in Morse code, Jim located a legislator seated in the back of the chamber when only given the title of a bill the man had recently introduced as a way of describing him. (I wonder how many legislators would have been able to perform so well, if asked to do so on that day.)

Jim was sometimes remarkable for what he could not do. Mary Burge was present one such day when she was a child, wearing a red dress with little white polka dots. When Jim was asked to "find the girl in the red dress," he walked around and surveyed the entire crowd, but made no selection. There were three girls wearing red dresses. He then was asked to find the girl in the red-and-white polka dot dress, which he did not do. Two girls, including Mary, were wearing red-and-white polka dot dresses. When asked to find the girl with the red-and-white polka dot dress and a red-and-white polka dot ribbon in her hair, Jim correctly selected the other little girl. Many years later Mary Burge was interviewed on camera about the incident and said, "Jim's eyes were different from other dogs; when you looked into them, they went forever."

Another famous case of Jim refusing to act was when Jim and VanArsdale were invited to do a demonstration for a class studying ancient Greek at Missouri University. Sam suggested the students write a question in Greek on a piece of paper and present it to Jim. When the paper was placed before the dog, Jim looked at it, but would not budge. VanArsdale began to get embarrassed by the lack of response from his generally cooperative dog, so he asked someone to translate the question for him so he might figure out why they had gotten no response. The students had tried to trick the pair by giving Jim a paper that only contained the letters of the Greek alphabet.

Jim was written up in *Ripley's Believe It or Not, Field and Stream, Outdoor Life, Missouri Ruralist, Missouri Life,* and the *Kansas City Star.* The *New York Times* offered to bring Sam with Jim to meet President Roosevelt in Washington, but for unstated reasons VanArsdale declined. He turned down more than $100,000 for a year-long cross-country tour with Jim and a reported $665,000 for one year of using Jim to make movies in Hollywood. Responding to the Hollywood offer, Sam VanArsdale stated simply, "I feel that Jim's powers are beyond my comprehension, and I do not care to commercialize them in any way."

After Jim's fame spread nationwide, the VanArsdales took a family vacation one winter to Florida. Although Sam reportedly made it a point of honor not to bet on any of the horses Jim picked to win a race (and his selections were seldom even known before the races were done), a man who was being paid to walk the dog apparently began to win a lot of money at the racetrack and supposedly gave the credit to Jim. VanArsdale received an anonymous warning his dog might disappear, so the family hastily cut their vacation short and returned to Missouri.

Throughout most of his life, Jim was known simply as "Jim," but invariably a whole host of adjectives were attached to him by writers who found, then, as I do now, how difficult a task it is to adequately describe what he seemed to be. In August 1935, two years before his death, and after a demonstration he gave at the Kemmerer Hotel in Kemmerer, Wyoming, the editor for the *Gazette of Kemmerer* wrote an article simply titled, "Wonder Dog Was Here Wednesday." That will now and forever be the title that will stick on Jim like a tick.

In that memorable piece C. W. Brandon began,

Jim, the wonder dog, who sees all and knows all, was in Kemmerer Wednesday evening and the tales told of this marvelous animal by those who witnessed the exhibition called for loud guffaws of ridicule by those who hadn't seen and could not believe. In fact some of them were called liars.

"As an example of his super canine instinct, Ivan S. Jones walked into the lobby of the Kemmerer Hotel and a query was written on a piece of paper, 'Who is the county and prosecuting attorney in this county?' The dog looked at the paper and walked over and put his paw on Mr. Jones' knee. It was equally facile for him to distinguish between Chevrolets and Fords. He could read signs, understand Morse code, and understand four languages. Some dog! But it is true, for the writer was there with the others.

Kemmerer is proud of its link to Jim, and a recent article, more than seventy-five years after Jim visited the town, closed with the words,

If the *Gazette* never gets to interview a U. S. President, or a famous celebrity, or never earns the distinction of winning the

Wyoming Press Association award for Newspaper of the Year, at least we can say that *The Gazette* has gone down in history as being the publication that gave Jim, the Wonder Dog his famous nickname . . . a tail-waggin' fact that we are mighty proud of!

I was taught to avoid ending a sentence with a preposition, like the one above, but I also learned you can always tack on a "Doggonit!" or the word for a female dog.

On March 18, 1937, Sam took Jim for a car ride from the town of Marshall, where they had lived for several years, to Lake of the Ozarks, where Sam planned to do a little fishing. When they arrived, Jim ran a short distance, but then suddenly collapsed. Sam drove frantically to an animal hospital he trusted in Sedalia, but once on the examination table Jim drew only two more breaths and died. VanArsdale requested his beloved canine friend be granted permission for burial in the family plot at the Ridge Park Cemetery in Marshall, but the request was denied because the people in charge declared, "a dog does not possess a soul." Jim was therefore buried in a special casket, just outside the cemetery gates. Ironically, the cemetery has since been expanded to include the ground where Jim was buried, so dog and master are in a sense united again. (Any Jim fan would suppose Jim knew this would happen, all along.) His grave is the most visited in the cemetery, and few of the people who come there to see it express any doubt about where Jim is now.

Dead these many years, Jim still stirs wonder and even controversy at times. Following an admiring blog post on a fun spot titled *From the Shadows* in 2007, an anonymous responder commented, "My mother grew up in Marshall and my little brother is buried in the same cemetery. I think it is creepy and want nothing to do with black magic. I find it ironic that he was born in Louisiana. The bible [sic] makes it clear that these type [sic] of gifts are not from God."

In 2012 a raucous scene ensued when a proposed bill to designate Jim Missouri's State Historic Dog came up against two competing bills, one most notably featuring Old Drum, the famous dog who was first ever to be called "man's best friend," and whose statue now stands in front of the courthouse in Warrensburg. The hearing grew so contentious the committee chair said no bill would be sent to the full House for debate that year. In 2013 a compromise was worked out whereby each famous dog received state recognition. (Good job guys and gals. Now let's see what kind of compromises you can cobble together on education legislation.)

Jim the Wonder Dog has a park dedicated to his memory in Marshall, on the site of the former Ruff Hotel (honest), which Sam VanArsdale managed when he moved back to Marshall from Sedalia in the mid-1930s. On that very ground Jim performed many of the feats for which he is so famous, and today you can follow a series of plaques describing his extraordinary abilities. He was also featured on the Animal Planet television series *Animal Legends* a few years back.

Jim, being modest, would probably not have cared. But given a bright fall day, with a nip in the air and the scent of pheasant or quail wafting out over the meadows, Jim would have sprung to the ready when his owner reached for his gun and whistled a come along. For most bird dogs that is communication enough, and they respond in total joy, tails wagging with unbounded enthusiasm. But for Jim there was apparently also some far deeper sense of understanding with his owner and perhaps all of mankind. From where his wisdom came, nobody seems to know.

CHAPTER 2

Tempus Fugit While a Cave Keeps Its Secrets

Each year tens of thousands of casual tourists enjoy driving to visit or just pass through the pretty little city of Neosho in Southwest Missouri. Aptly nicknamed the "Gateway to the Ozarks," the quiet community does indeed seem to serve as a perfect welcoming host to travelers entering the region from the dry flatlands of Oklahoma, sunny Kansas, and points west. Nestled on tree-covered hills with abundant springs, the lovely setting gives a hint of the beauty that lies beyond throughout the Ozark Mountains with their many sparkling rivers and lush green valleys. "City of Springs" and "The Flower Box City" are other picturesque names by which Neosho is known. Driving from the nearby quaint town square or the popular Neosho National Fish Hatchery to quiet, sun-dappled Big Spring Park in the middle of town, you might think you were entering an ideal urban Eden. But hidden somewhere beneath the idyllic grounds of Big Spring Park lies the lost entrance to a forbidding cave with a dark and dangerous past.

You can buy a colorful postcard of the famous Neosho floral clock that has kept time at the park entrance for most of the last fifty years. Unfortunately for those who love it, the huge hands of the clock, which swept for countless hours across the clock's 17-foot diameter, repeatedly proved to be too great a temptation for rambunctious children in the daytime and bored vandals at night. Sitting on the hands of the clock and attempting to turn them backwards or stealing the hands completely resulted in unreasonable costs to repair and maintain the floral clock, which is one of fewer than one hundred in existence worldwide. When first installed in 1967, the clock face was adorned with three thousand living, blooming plants. Later, as upkeep became problematic and costly, that number was cut in half. How many plants comprise the clock face these days is unknown, and the issue of whether to repair the clock mechanism yet again has become a recurring subject for hot debate at city meetings. But that disturbing dilemma is just a tempest in a teapot compared to the controversy swirling around Big Spring Park's darker secrets. The decades of hours kept thus far by the floral clock when it was working are just a spark in the dark compared to the years of fears, hopes, and fantasies covered up in Abbott's lost Civil War Cave.

The land that became Neosho was first settled by Europeans around 1833. The town would not be incorporated until much later in 1878. *Neosho* is an Osage Indian word that means "clear, cold water." That fact is notable because the wider region around Neosho was known by the settlers for many years as "Six Bulls," which is said to have been a bastardization of the name "Six Boils," representing the six dependable water sources located there, including four good creeks and two large rivers. To distinguish the springs of Neosho as such, within a region of abundant waters, must have carried considerable meaning to native inhabitants who were highly aware of their local surroundings, as such knowledge was essential to survival itself.

One can read accounts of early Spanish explorers traveling through the area looking for legendary gold mines and enslaving some of the Indians they found there to dig for them, before the first permanent European settlers came and began mining in the area for both lead and zinc. Some of the earliest mentions of the cave at Big Spring Park in written and oral histories are rumors that early slaveholders would use portions of the cave to confine their slaves to keep them from running away at night.

The small piece of land that became Big Spring Park was later a limestone quarry before the Civil War, and remnants of old lime kilns have been discovered within the park's boundaries. The resources of lime and limestone, plus the abundance of fresh, clear water, meant substantial building could be done at the site and nearby, so the little outpost prospered and grew.

On August 3, 1854, an act of Congress allocated $17,000 to establish an express mail route between Neosho and Albuquerque, New Mexico, in an attempt to improve communication between the United States to the east and territories acquired as a result of the Mexican American War. The experiment did not prove profitable, however, and less than a year later the service was changed to run from Independence, Missouri, to Stockton, California, through Albuquerque. One more shift occurred in 1860, creating the famous Pony Express route that ran from St. Joseph, Missouri, to Sacramento, California. Had the easternmost station of the Pony Express been created and maintained in Neosho, it is quite possible the region might have remained more loyal to the Union during the Civil War than it did.

Unlike much of the rest of the Ozarks, southern sympathizers who were slaveholders held sway in and around Neosho for much of the Civil War. On October 21, 1861, Governor (and Confederate sympathizer) Claiborne Jackson met with a group of like-minded Missouri legislators in Neosho, after being driven out of Jefferson City by encroaching Union troops. The routed officials voted on October 28 to secede from the Union while under the protection of Confederate General Sterling Price, whose troops held the high ground surrounding Neosho. In short order Missouri was accepted as the twelfth state of the Confederacy. You will thus hear claims Neosho served, for one week, as the state capital of Missouri.

The victory was pyrrhic, however, because pro-Union troops deposed Governor Jackson and set up Governor Hamilton R. Gamble to restore Missouri to the Union cause. General Price fled south out of Missouri, and the Battle of Pea Ridge (Arkansas) cemented the Union's hold over most of Missouri. Confederate incursions continued to keep the area around Neosho in limbo during much of the rest of the war, however. Neosho was occupied alternately by Union and Confederate troops numerous times. The cave at Big Spring served as a supply depot at different times for both armies.

General Joseph Shelby staged raids throughout extreme southwest Missouri and as far north as Marshall, at one point burning much of Neosho and capturing the Union garrison there. Union troops counterattacked and drove out the Confederates, who made little effort to hold the ground. At some point the Union troops became convinced rebels were using the depths of Big Spring Cave as a hideout from which to stage their raids, so they blasted the entrance to the cave. Some old-timers said as many as two hundred Confederate troops were sealed inside, along with a large shipment of Confederate gold. Others insist if there were soldiers inside when the cave was sealed at the front entrance, the hillsides were so honeycombed with caves that anyone inside who knew the layout of the cave system would have had no trouble escaping in secret.

After the Civil War, Neosho entered a time of peace and prosperity. Agriculture flourished. After the phylloxera louse destroyed most of the vineyards of France, Spain, and Portugal in 1882, it was discovered that Swiss winemaker Hermann Jaeger's grapevines growing just a little east of Neosho were resistant to the pest. He shipped seventeen boxcars of his rootstock to Europe, an act that

NEOSHO AREA CHAMBER OF COMMERCE

For many years Neosho's Flower Clock received more time and attention from city employees than the Lost Civil War Cave, which is hidden, with a forgotten entrance somewhere nearby.

is credited with saving the European wine industry and earning Jaeger the Legion of Honor from France. The favorable publicity that resulted helped to lay the groundwork for a robust nursery industry that grew up in and around Neosho and lasted throughout the better part of the twentieth century. Jaeger's fate, however, was not so sunny. Facing financial ruin in the face of America's push toward Prohibition, he moved to Joplin. Soon after, he left home, telling his wife he was headed to Neosho. Several days later she received a letter, written by him, postmarked in Kansas City, stating, "When you read this, I will no longer be alive," and predicting his body would never be found. So far as we know, he was 100 percent correct.

In the same way other notable Civil War cities across the United States have put their violent pasts behind them and in perspective, Neosho steadily grew with happier things in mind. The city proudly proclaims itself the once home of such notable Americans as botanist, educator, and inventor George Washington Carver, artist and muralist Thomas Hart Benton, and ragtime composer and performer James Scott. During World War II and after, nearby Camp Crowder south of town served as training ground and home to untold thousands of men and women army recruits, for whom the pretty little city of Neosho represented a bit of hometown America and perhaps a symbol of what they were fighting to protect.

Camp Crowder and Neosho entered even more into the American psyche in the 1960s when Army veterans and fellow comedians Carl Reiner and Dick Van Dyke made those locales the settings where the fictional television couple Rob and Laura Petrie met and married on the *Dick Van Dyke Show,* when Rob was in the Army and Laura (played by Mary Tyler Moore) was a USO dancer. Camp Crowder must have been an awfully funny place back then, because famed cartoonist Mort Walker also used the notoriously flood-prone Army base as the fictional setting of "Camp Swampy," in his popular *Beetle Bailey* cartoon strip.

In 1957 Neosho was designated an "All American City" by *Look* magazine. In a beautification project second to none, residents of the town constructed two hundred flower boxes from donated lumber and received four hundred barrels from the Pet Milk Company. Those containers were all placed around town and filled with colorful flowering plants provided at discount by Neosho's several famous nurseries. Additionally, trash cans and parking meters throughout the city received a beauty treatment with more blossoming plants. The attention of *LOOK* magazine's writers, editors, and photographers when they came was entirely focused on what was so eye-catching at eye level. No one at *LOOK* magazine back then was interested in digging up Neosho's Civil War secrets or writing about a different kind of colorful past.

When Camp Crowder was deactivated, some of its facilities and Neosho became famous as the home of America's rocket engine program, where engines for Atlas, Thor, and Saturn missiles, plus Mercury and Gemini rocket engines, were assembled and tested. But even while all that noise was going on above ground, the secrets of Neosho's lost Civil War cave were lying silent and hidden from view.

Within a few years after the Civil War, curious residents had reopened an entrance to Big Spring Cave for a brief time, probably in search of the legendary Confederate gold hoard rumored to be buried there. Whatever the cause, amateur spelunkers, both young and old, began exploring the cave with the primitive equipment they had available. Some reported becoming disoriented and lost in the vast cave system for extended periods of time.

In 1896 the young Abbott brothers famously went missing while exploring the cave and did not emerge for more than twenty-four hours. When the plight of the little boys was known, the town held an emergency meeting and sent two experienced spelunkers into the cave to look for them. Those men nearly became lost themselves. After another hasty discussion, everyone in town was sent home to bring back whatever string they could find. All the string the townsfolk could gather was tied together, and in that manner two balls of string about the size of basketballs were wound together. By unraveling the string as they again probed the vast labyrinth of the cave, the rescuers were able to find both boys unharmed and bring them out safely.

As a result of the Abbott brothers' misadventure, the fearful town fathers decided the dangerous cave would be "closed in a permanent manner," so no other individuals would be lost. They must have done a terrific job. The cave was sealed and the park more extensively landscaped, so with the passage of time almost no one was left who remembered exactly where the entrance had been located.

Opinions about whether the cave should have been closed must have been as fiercely opposed as the soldiers who fought in the Civil War. Many of the citizens in town insisted the site marked a sacred Confederate mass grave. Others wanted to see if the cave really did contain as much as two million dollars in gold. Doubtless there were those who just saw the cave as a fun place to crawl around and explore. In 1925 park superintendent Robert D. Mullins excavated at the east side of the park in an attempt to find the hidden entrance to the cave. He found evidence of the old lime kilns before being ordered by the mayor to cease. In 1947 a subsequent park superintendent tried again to locate the entrance to the cave, in order to open it to the public, but he likewise was ordered to halt his search by another mayor who was hostile to the idea.

Despite their ordeal as children, at the end of their lives the bachelor brothers E. M. and J. W. Abbott must have been solidly on the side of the "openers," for as old men they included Neosho generously in their wills. Together they left $30,000 in trust to the city with the stated intention that the interest generated should be used for park maintenance, a driveway entrance, and expenses to reopen the cave as a tourist attraction. Some geologists who were asked to consider the proposal suggested the cave system under Neosho might rival Carlsbad Caverns in New Mexico. Perhaps to emphasize their point, the Abbotts also left the city of Neosho a building on the square, which was sold for the revenue, and a 147-acre farm in Oklahoma, which is profitably rented out to farmers for crops to this day.

For all their trouble and largesse, the Abbott brothers have been rewarded posthumously with a small monument that memorializes their brief disappearance underground and names the cave officially for them. A pretty little Grecian-style wading pool graces one side of the park and an arched footbridge spans a little stream. The only hint of the cave system visible today is Stair Step Cave, a small grotto tucked beneath the cliff face that serves as a dramatic border rising above the park.

The last serious attempt to find and open the entrance to Abbott Cave was conducted by Jim Cole more than a dozen years ago when he was city manager. A good twenty years prior to that, Cole had been the city's director of public works when Dr. Robert Layton of Neosho approached him with the research he had collected related to the Civil War cave. Cole needed little encouragement, but their discussions nudged him to conduct what eventually became over 350 interviews with elderly residents and their descendants, in order to plumb the mysteries surrounding the lost cave.

"I always liked caves, but they were not my top priority," Cole told a reporter modestly in the year 2000, when news of his probing gained some fairly widespread publicity. Gradually the possibility of a significant find underground caused the hunt for the truth about Abbott Cave and its whereabouts to become Cole's "#1 Hobby," as the reporter described it. Eventually Cole's position with the city made him the trustee of the Abbott estate legacy, so he had access to some money and equipment to apply to the cause.

Whispers of Confederate gold grew louder and talk of potential tourist dollars caught the attention of those who never bought the idea of buried treasure. Any hint of missing mass graves of Civil War soldiers will always get quite a bit of attention, with some folks eager to bring in forensic anthropologists, and others who demand the bodies of the dead be left undisturbed. As low key as Cole had been about his searches, there were nevertheless reportedly people in town who refused to talk to him at all because of his work.

In 1999 Cole conducted four exploratory digs in the park that led to the discovery of what he described as "a small cavern, 5' high and about 125' in diameter." He advanced a theory to a reporter for the *Joplin Globe*, saying, "I think 4 or 5 caves in the park all tie together in the south."

Numerous residents with old houses on the steep hill above the park and elsewhere around town have described evidence of connections to the cave system from their properties. Some regard these cave chambers and chimneys as nuisances and have closed them completely, while others hint that secret entrances may exist in their cellars and basements. Understandably, few land owners want strangers prowling around their property in the daytime, or muddy spelunkers emerging from their basements in the middle of the night. One such resident advanced the theory that if a massive cave system once existed beneath Neosho, perhaps today it has been filled with a flood of mud.

The pendulum seems to have swung back on the search to find and open Abbott Cave. You will see no evidence of serious digging if you visit Big Spring Park these days, unless it is some park employee planting a dogwood, or a lady with a trowel fixing the flower border surrounding the floral clock. Jim Cole has retired from public service, and you are lucky if you can catch him at home when he is not out tending his cattle on his place near another town where there is no talk of hunting for lost Civil War caves.

When I talked to Jim Cole, he claimed a bit of deafness, so I could not tell for sure if he heard all my questions, or just heard things he didn't want to discuss. He seems to bear no ill will toward the people who opposed his searches or any frustration with his successors in city government who have neglected to carry on his quest.

With a relaxed, sanguine attitude I find admirable, Jim Cole seems at peace with the notion no amount of ruckus aboveground caused by the unanswered questions and controversies surrounding Abbott Cave will disturb the secrets locked within its dark depths. Meanwhile, most families eating at the picnic tables scattered about Big Spring Park seem unaware of what lies underground just a few feet away. Tourists who drive in after noticing the floral clock or signs for the park often turn around and drive out without stopping, obviously thinking there is little there for them to do or see. Indeed, residents of this quiet little town seem content to keep it that way.

CHAPTER 3

This Missouri Hideout Was Not a Jesse James Cave

D o you want to know a secret? Alton, Missouri, was not the obvious choice for a quick getaway in the early 1960s.

Many people need convincing it ever was at all. Those four huge celebrities could have gone anywhere they wanted for some R & R on a couple of days off: New York, Chicago . . . even Disneyland. But what they really wanted was peace and quiet. Slow down. Get back.

Put yourself back in time, in their black, pointy-toed shoes. It was a beginning.

The year is 1964. Your band just finished filming its first full-length feature film, followed by a whirlwind "World Tour," a few gigs back home in merry old England, and finally a month-long tour across North America. This thirty-day tour you are on with the Yanks stateside will net you lads a record profit of $7.5 million in today's dollars. But it's been a string of hard days' nights just about eight days a week, and you've been working like, well, dogs.

The Beatles were understandably so tired from turning the world on its head, seemingly overnight. The enormity of what they were accomplishing could scarcely have begun to sink in with them. Beginning as phenomenal entertainers, they would soon also rank among the most influential poets, philosophers, and political activists for generations of people, young and old, the world over. Clearly life would never be the same for John Lennon, Paul McCartney, George Harrison, and Ringo Starr. Now at the tail end of their zigzag tour of North America, they had just thirty-six hours off before a final charity concert in New York City at the Paramount Theatre. From there it was a long, tiring flight back home, to where literally years of bookings and commitments awaited them. They would never get to enjoy such a quintessentially bucolic American vacation together again.

Imagine. John Lennon, Paul McCartney, George Harrison, and Ringo Starr. They toured twenty-five cities, giving thirty-four concerts in thirty days. The Fab Four might not qualify as a "boy band" by today's standards, but in some ways the young men were the first boy band when their careers took off in the early 1960s. And no matter how energetic a group of young singers might be, the crazy schedule, the long hours, and the wild lifestyle they had been living for months would cause anyone to feel played out. Earlier on the American tour the band more or less squandered their first three scheduled days off. But not all of it could be considered their fault.

August 24 was spent hiding from their legions of fans in a rented house in the swank Bel Air section of Los Angeles,

California. (John Lennon did manage to sneak out for a few hours with road manager Neil Aspinall and publicist Derek Taylor, but their little foray ended abruptly when John was recognized and they were forced to give the screaming crowds the slip and flee back to their Bel Air lair.)

A week later found the Beatles and their small entourage again holed up on a day off, this time clear across the country at a luxury hotel in Cape May, New Jersey. There, the band's whereabouts was no secret, so mobs of hysterical fans surrounding the hotel made even a walk along the beach unthinkable. Paul managed to put a call through to Elvis Presley, and they talked, but the five men would not meet in person until the following year.

August 9 was to have been an overnight in Montreal, Canada, following two concerts there, and before a planned day off in Jacksonville, Florida. Few realized, however, the group had received death threats from French-Canadian separatists, so they performed their two concerts for a total of twenty one thousand fans while under the watchful eyes (and rifles) of police sharpshooters. The experience left the boys a little shaken, so they cut that leg of their tour short and boarded a flight to Jacksonville, only to be told en route a hurricane was causing them to be diverted to Key West. Before landing they were warned the runway might not be long enough for such a large plane. (It was, but barely.)

Perhaps it is no surprise then that the lads from Liverpool chose to spend their third day off on August 10 in a cheap Key West motel, where they got royally drunk. Sir Paul said years later they had little else to do but drink while they were hiding out from fans on the most famous of the Florida Keys. As he has told the story in interviews, the band mates got so schnockered in the little motel they ended up hugging, crying, and telling each other how much they loved each other, even if they never said anything about it at any other time. "Northern men" is how Paul described their awkward attitude toward displays of affection before the Beatles discovered love is all you need.

Just when it seemed their plans for a little holiday time while in America could not go wrong again, one of the Beatles' remaining days off was bartered away by their famed and fabled über manager Brian Epstein. Chicago area businessman Charles O. Finley, new owner of the major league Athletics, then based in Kansas City, initially offered Epstein $50,000 if the Beatles would play a concert at Municipal Stadium to please his teenage daughter. Few people who knew him thought Charlie-O was really doing it solely to please his daughter, but when the Beatles said "no, no, no," the bidding became fierce, and Epstein finally convinced them to accept a record-setting offer of $150,000—six times the going rate for a single performance from top-tier talent in those days.

The Kansas City concert was not billed with any mention of Finley's daughter, but rather with the slogan, "Today's Beatles Fans Are Tomorrow's Baseball Fans." Charlie-O was not universally loved during his team's brief time in Kansas City, which some say is why the concert was the only one during the entire North American tour where the Beatles did not play to a sold-out crowd. They attracted a respectable audience topping 20,000, but the stadium could seat 35,000, and Finley reportedly lost between $50,000 and $100,000 on the deal.

Money don't get everything, it's true, but after another concert in Dallas on September 18, the Beatles laughed all the way to the banks of the Eleven Point River at Alton, Missouri. The group was heady with the knowledge they had just earned the highest per-minute performance salary in history, as part of an already record-breaking rock' n' roll tour. The band and their little entourage were ready to blow off a wee bit of steam. (Is it possible some of their giggles were also due to a now famous meeting the group had with Bob Dylan in a smoke-filled New York hotel room just three weeks before?) Whatever their reasons, John, Paul, George, and Ringo each remarked over the ensuing years how much they enjoyed their mini-vacation at the Pigman Ranch just outside Alton, Missouri.

Reed Pigman was an aviation pioneer who owned the profitable American Flyers Airline Corporation that had been chartered to fly the Beatles around North America on their summer tour. Somewhere along the way, Pigman convinced the Beatles and manager Brian Epstein his ranch outside Alton would be the best place to relax and enjoy a rural American vacation and some good old home cooking. Pigman and his family used the place as a getaway and vacation home when they weren't living in Texas or flying all over the world. The place was pretty fancy by local standards, with extensive landscaping, a swimming pool, and many other amenities only dreamed of by local folks. But make no mistake: Pigman Ranch was a working ranch, the largest in Missouri. It took four families in residence, plus other employees, just to run the place when the owners weren't even there.

After their concert in Dallas on September 18, the band and their crew flew in their regular charter to Walnut Ridge, Arkansas, just south of the Missouri border, from where Pigman would fly the Fab Four plus Epstein, Neil Aspinall, and Derek Taylor the rest of the way in his small, private, twin engine plane. On the first leg of the trip, at one minute after midnight, Paul got on the intercom and announced it was Brian's thirtieth birthday, so the friends sang happy birthday (imagine what an original tape of that rendition would be worth today) and presented Epstein with gifts of fine water glasses and an antique telephone. The gesture of friendship and the stress-free hospitality extended to the group by the locals in Missouri prompted Epstein to tell *Mersey Beat* magazine a couple of weeks later their stay at the Pigman Ranch was his happiest time in America.

For fretful George, however, the happy time and relaxation wouldn't begin until the little seven-seater used on the second leg of the trip landed safely on the grass airfield. "It was so like Buddy Holly, that one," George reminisced for *The Beatles Anthology* years later. He described Reed Pigman with a little map on his knee in the darkness with a flashlight in the cockpit, saying, "Oh, I don't know where we are," as they flew through the mountains with Pigman wiping repeatedly to clear the windshield so he could see out. When they finally put down, it was on a tiny unpaved airstrip with tin can luminaries for runway lights. (George, you don't know how lucky you are, Boy. Pigman would die in a plane crash less than two years later, after suffering a heart attack while transporting personnel for the government.) Finally at the ranch, and unbeknownst to any but a handful of folks on an entire continent who had gone completely Beatles crazy, the Liverpool musicians got to ride horses (some say for the first time ever), fish in the large stocked pond, and race around the barnyard in a barebones go cart. Brian Epstein's spin on their adventures for *Mersey Beat* was that

> the Beatles, though not devoted to sport, took readily to the saddle, however, and fought majestically for three hours with four high-spirited farm horses, fording the river, climbing steep rocky banks, and emerging without a fall but several bruises. So much did Paul enjoy riding that he awoke at 7 am on Sunday for a further attempt which proved even more painful than the first.

Epstein was clearly a master of public relations.

Locals will tell you (and pictures prove) the horses saddled for the Beatles were not the high-spirited mounts Epstein described, but rather the kind of safe, predictable old nags preferred by ranchers for their unseasoned guests, so greenhorn visitors would not be thrown onto the hard ground or into a cattle tank. The lads nevertheless enthusiastically donned cowboy hats over their famously long locks, to accessorize their exotic British attire, and proceeded to let their steeds take them all about the premises, at whatever speed the horses deemed necessary. Their revolutionary hairstyles were short by the standards that would soon prevail all around the world for decades, but at the time they were freakishly long and eccentric to most of the adults in America. Ironically, it gives some of their photos from the vacation an atmosphere more authentic to old-time cowboys, as opposed to the crew cuts, flat tops, and greasy Elvis pompadours that still dominated back in Alton at the time.

Ringo got a hold of a large pair of cap pistols with holsters somewhere, which he hung from a tooled leather belt emblazoned with the name "Ringo." Many have said they believe the belt at least, and the toy guns, perhaps, were a gift sent to the drummer by none other than Elvis himself. Reed Pigman Jr., who was fourteen at the time, said later the famous drummer and country music fan wore his cap pistols almost the entire time the Beatles were at the ranch, and he used them to shoot at "everything in sight." Even a fourteen-year-old seemed to think the joke wore thin after a while. But that was four years before the Beatles famously sang John's tongue-in-cheek song, "Happiness Is a Warm Gun." Ironically, in 1980 John Lennon would be shot and killed by a delusional fan.

There must have also been some Hard Day's Night–style slapstick moments while on the ranch, as well, because at one point one of the Beatles (most say it was George) knocked a door clear off the ranch manager's truck while tooling around in a 1960 Ford

Fairlane, loaned to the Brits for use just on the 13,000-acre spread. Baby, someone must have regretted saying, "You can drive my car."

Debbie Sallings was barely a teenager at the time, but she remembers vividly being lucky enough to ride with Shirley Barton and her daughters past the front gates and almost a quarter mile up to the main house in order to see the Beatles in person. Initially friends of the family and people who worked at the ranch were allowed in, but as word spread and a small crowd gathered, almost no one else was admitted. Debbie describes seeing the Beatles on horseback in the driveway as they drove up. There wasn't much conversation, because the locals had an Ozarks' respect for privacy (and what adolescent girl can think of something clever and sophisticated to say when suddenly confronted with the four most famous young men in the world?). But Debbie does remember Ringo asking, "Paul, have you got my ciggies?" So apparently the lads weren't yet rolling their own as part of their cowboy adventure.

When Debbie returned later in the day, the crowd had swollen and she noticed cars from as far away as Tennessee; but security had been beefed up and no one without a good reason was being admitted. She laughs at her memories of four older, enterprising teens commandeering a boat after dark and navigating the Eleven Point River to a place from where they could sneak onto the grounds and peek in the windows. The furtive four friends (three guys and a girl) were rewarded with the sight of the Beatles and members of their entourage playing poker in one of the bedrooms.

COURTESY OF THE DETHROW FAMILY

Mary Dethrow may look like she is going to slap that ciggie out of Paul's mouth as publicist Derek Taylor and her mother, Thelma Roy, look on, but she was just giving directions to the fishing pond out back.

Bob Gum, now deceased, told Debbie afterward the British singers were half-watching and listening to the *Gene Williams Country Television Show*, which had debuted on KAIT in Jonesboro, Arkansas, less than a year earlier. *Country Junction* was the real deal for anyone who followed country music, and that night Gum and his friends couldn't help but notice the Beatles were listening to the Buck Owens hit, "Act Naturally," which was just coming off a long run on the Country charts. You'll probably never convince anybody from Alton that when Ringo covered "Act Naturally" for the Beatles in 1965, they weren't trying to recapture just a little of the atmosphere of their adventures playing cowboys in Missouri.

Another eyewitness to the Beatles' little cowboy adventure is Brenda Ledgerwood, who was eleven at the time, and daughter of Roy Dethrow Jr., ranch foreman. The Dethrow family lived on the ranch, and John, Paul, and Ringo autographed Brenda's clarinet case for her. Even today Brenda remembers the Beatles sitting in front of the large white barn, joking and laughing as they prepared to ride the horses.

Brenda takes exception to accounts that years later have characterized Pigman Ranch as a "dude ranch," implying it was some sort of pampered vacation spot where the Beatles might have been attended to by hospitality staff. The workers on the Pigman Ranch attended instead to a huge herd of prized Holsteins and the other jobs it took to keep the whole place running smoothly. Most of the ranch hands didn't any more than pause from their daily duties when they were interrupted by the Beatles' brief stay. Brenda tells of how Paul and Derek Taylor came to her house to borrow her brother's fishing pole, and were sent off by her mother, who just pointed them in the direction of the pond behind their house, obviously figuring these men surely knew how to bait a hook and cast a line, no matter where they came from, or how famous they were. I can almost imagine her admonishing them, "And you boys be sure to close that gate after you, or I'll have to cut me a switch!"

Over the years there have been many little impromptu Beatles tribute events and musical gatherings in Alton, attended mostly by locals who have connections to people who were around at the time of the little-known visit. Kids whose parents weren't even born at the time nevertheless have fun covering their favorite Beatles songs and imagining what might have happened if only they were around back then. The Alton Community Foundation is planning a big Missouri BeatlesFest on September 12 and 13, 2014, to celebrate the fiftieth anniversary of the Fab Four's foray into the Missouri Ozarks. George's sister, Louise Harrison, has arranged for a special performance by the Liverpool Legends tribute band she produces in Branson, and locals are assembling a "Beatles Museum" with memorabilia from their visit on display, Beatles movies playing, and local folks recounting their memories of when John, Paul, George, and Ringo escaped their fanatical fans and enjoyed a couple of days of being just a bunch of blokes on a real ranch in America.

Do you suppose they called it "Missour-ee" or "Missour-ah" with their Liverpool accents?

CHAPTER 4

The Lost Silver Mine and the Mystery of Yocum Dollars

One of the most colorful characters living in the Missouri Ozarks is Artie Ayres. Ozark native, author, landowner, sometime speculator, onetime politician, and (in the best sense of the phrase) hillbilly entrepreneur, Artie seems to have had a grand time throughout his long life.

Next time you are visiting Branson (as everyone eventually does), drive across the Table Rock Lake Dam and look at the deep water just up along the north shore. It was in a log home built by his family on land there, now long submerged by the waters of the White River, that Artie was born February 4, 1926. It was Artie who gave people fits when he changed the name of the town Lakeview to Branson West in order to capitalize on the incredible publicity Branson received when the so-called "Live Entertainment Capital of the World" boomed in the early 1990s. It was Artie who quietly kept Walmart executives tied up for months, when they desperately wanted a piece of the land he owns not far from Branson for a supercenter. He still owns some of the prettiest land in the Ozarks. And he wrote one of the most enthralling historical accounts of what this tourist-crazed part of Missouri used to be like.

Artie Ayres's book, *Traces of Silver*, was published in 1982. The slim volume is currently out of print, but like almost everything else interesting he has ever done, Ayres reserves the right to do it again. I hope he will. When I could not locate my copy of his book, I visited several local libraries, but each time I was told the same thing: "We've had several copies, but people steal them, and every time we get a new one they disappear." (I finally found my copy, and I'm not loaning it out.)

The book *Traces of Silver* tells many stories, but the thread woven throughout is the tale of the Lost Silver Mine of the Ozarks and the Yocum silver dollars supposedly minted there. The heroes are the hill people (many of them Artie's relatives), whose lives were once as remote and hidden from the rest of the world as any lost treasure could ever be. Read his book and when you walk the same ground he writes about, where now so many tourists come to frolic and hear musicians play, you'll find yourself gazing at little valleys, wondering if that could be the place where the Lost Silver Mine lies hidden.

The Ayres telling of the legend begins, as most others on the subject do, about the time in 1816 when three men named Yoachum entered the territory now known as Ozark Mountain

Country. The men were James (who had traveled, traded, and fur trapped here previously), his adult son Jacob, and James's brother Solomon. The men, better known by the names Jim, Jake, and Sol, lived near and among the Delaware Indians, who had been pushed progressively west, ahead of European settlers' westward expansion. The Delaware, themselves, were displacing the indigenous Osage Indians from what had been some of their seasonal hunting grounds, but soon all Indians would be unwelcome here, as more white settlers came into the area and crowded them out.

But the Yoachum men lived peaceably with the Delaware, Jim even taking a Delaware woman as his wife. (Jim's first wife, Jake's mother, had died when the boy was still young.) The Indians taught the Yoachums many survival skills they needed, and the Yoachums found a number of ways to make themselves helpful to the Indians in return.

Henry Rowe Schoolcraft, the noted geographer, geologist, and ethnologist, briefly cites encounters he and a companion had with the "Yochems" (as he spelled their oft-morphed surname), and in so doing ranked those men among the most admirable of any he met in the Ozarks. Sometimes referred to as "the Lewis and Clark of the Ozarks" for his detailed journals of travels through the region, Schoolcraft wrote prose that was elegant and old-fashioned, yet often very funny and tellingly to the point. His description of a gathering of the average Ozarks backwoodsmen gives a good example of the general population over which the Yoachum men excelled:

41

Yesterday arrived several neighbors and friends in their canoes, who came to town to trade, making a party of twelve or fourteen in all. Whiskey soon began to circulate freely, and by the time they had unloaded their canoes, we began plainly to discover that a scene of riot and drinking was to follow. Of all this, we were destined to be unwilling witnesses; for as there was but one house, and that a very small one, necessity compelled us to pass the night together; but sleep was not to be obtained. Every mouth, hand and foot, were in motion. Some drank, some sang, some danced, a considerable proportion attempted all three together, and a scene of undistinguishable bawling and riot ensued. An occasional quarrel gave variety to the scene, and now and then, one drunker than the rest, fell sprawling upon the floor, and for a while remained quiet. We alone remained listeners to this grand exhibition of human noises, beastly intoxication, and mental and physical nastiness. We did not lie down to sleep, for that was dangerous. Thus the night rolled heavily on, and as soon as light could be discerned in the morning we joyfully embarked in our canoe, happy in having escaped bodily disfiguration, and leaving such as could stand, vociferating with all their might like some delirious man upon his dying bed, who makes one desperate effort to arise, and then falls back in death.

In my mind I can't help thinking this was an early nineteenth-century version of that Three Dog Night classic song, "Mama Told Me Not to Come." By way of contrast, Schoolcraft and his

friend spent a night with Sol Yoachum, which he described as having gone a bit better:

> As the shades of night overtook us, a hunter's cabin was
> descried on the left shore, where a landing was made. It proved
> to be occupied by a person of the name Yochem, who readily
> gave us permission to remain for the night . . . He regaled us
> hospitably with wild viands, and, among other meats, the bea-
> ver's tail – a dish for epicures.

A day or two later, Schoolcraft and his companion encountered Jake Yoachum, and they were equally impressed by him,
seemingly without realizing this was the nephew of their previous host: "We embarked and descended the river six miles to a Mr.
Jacob Yochem's, who received us with hospitality, and added no
little, by his conversation, to our local lore."

It is a small wonder, therefore, that as Artie Ayres recounted,
the Delaware Indians remained friendly with the Yoachums until
they were again forced to move by the government from the lands
they had been granted in Southwest Missouri. Jim's Delaware wife,
Winonah, was able to remain, but many thousands were sent to
live on land up around Kansas City. According to Ayres, due to
friendships forged over time, some of the Delaware braves decided
to trade to the Yoachums the secret location of their silver mine,
which people thought had been the source of mysterious silver
beads early settlers saw the Indians wearing.

Blankets, soap and two horses were given to the Indians in exchange for the Silver Mine. The Indians were very interested in the soap as they had observed the Yoachums washing their hands with it. Their dirty hands would be white when they finished, and some of the Indians thought that this was the reason these white men had lighter skin color than their own . . .

The three brothers built . . . directly across the valley from the mine entrance, so one of them could guard its entrance at all times. Later, they concluded that in order to keep the mine location a secret, they would build Jim's cabin directly in front of the opening and then fix a secret entrance from the house to the mine. Since his Indian wife spoke very little English it would be easy for them to keep its location a secret.

Ayres goes on to describe how the Yoachums further concealed the location of the mine from locals by making secretive trips away from home right before they intended to smelt the silver ore into dollars. Making sure they gave anyone following them "the slip," the returning men were thus thought to have been prospecting far away from home when they returned a few days later with bulging saddlebags.

It was not illegal to mint coins privately until 1862, so the Yoachums had no need to keep a secret of the fact they were making their own dollars. The last change in the spelling of their name came about, as Ayres tells it, because all the letters for "Yoachum" would not easily fit on a dollar, so the simple name "Yocum" was minted onto the coins and thus came into common usage. As to the source of their silver, Jim, Jake, and Sol didn't much care if people wanted to believe it came from a mine the Spanish explorer DeSoto was rumored to have found, a Delaware Indian discovery, or a cache at the end of a pale rainbow. The Yocums just didn't want anybody nosing around discovering their secrets.

Changes that came about with the Homestead Acts required so-called "squatters" who had moved onto lands in the public domain to eventually pay something to receive legal deeds for their property, regardless of whether they had made improvements to the land. The issue was highly controversial and widely ignored by the independent Ozarkers, but gradually settlers from the remote settlements began making their way to the Springfield Land Office to pay their fees and claim their legally deeded titles.

One of the first recorded incidents of Yocum dollars coming to the notice of government officials was supposedly when a settler attempted to pay his filing fee with Yocum trade coins. Ayres wrote the coins had been widely accepted in the wilderness, but the clerk suspected they might be counterfeit and initially refused to accept them. The rough individual from the White River Valley suggested the clerk might do well to accept the coinage rather than the consequences, so he left with his deed, but the clerk sent the coins to Washington for assay. Word came back from on high that the silver content was even higher than that of government-minted coins. The clerk was instructed to send all such coins to Washington and learn of the source.

Not long after, a government official made his way to the remote cabin of Jim Yocum and demanded to know the source of his silver. In a manner you cannot appreciate unless you have heard a hill person speak it, Jim pointed to the road the petty functionary had ridden in on and suggested he make a one-way trip back home. His instructions were quickly followed and no other government men were seen on the road again.

In Ayres's telling of the tale, tragedy struck sometime around 1846 or 1847. A mine collapse occurred, with Jim and Winonah inside the mine. As survival seemed impossible, Sol and Jake made no attempt at rescue, but instead further sealed the mine and concealed it. Returning to their wives and families, they initially expressed surprise Jim and Winonah had apparently not returned yet from a hunting trip. When enough time went by to cause alarm, Jake and Sol searched in vain with the others of the clan, knowing full well their relatives would never be found.

The two remaining men who knew the secret of the Lost Silver Mine discussed reopening the mine, but decided against it as too dangerous. Haunted by the tragic deaths of Jim and Winonah, the men moved their families to the mouth of the Kings River, where it empties into the White River. In 1849 gold was discovered at Sutter's Mill in California, and in 1850 Jake and Sol moved with part of their families west, to seek their fortunes there.

Artie Ayres continues the story in a more personal way, describing how his father, Ben, a "furriner" in the Ozarks, as the locals called him, came to be here. Ben Ayres disembarked with a buddy while riding a freight train through the Ozarks after leading a life of adventure on the cross-country rails. Artie wrote he has never been sure whether the men willingly stopped to appreciate the beauty of the Ozarks, or if a railroad employee might have encouraged them to leave the train hastily. Soon after, Ben met and married Artie's mom, Ella Fern Goodall, somewhat against her father's wishes. Ozarkers back then had a mistrust of suitors from elsewhere, who had not been tempered by the harsh conditions "local boys" had survived. To adequately explain, it is necessary to use words Henry Rowe Schoolcraft wrote of local youths:

> In their childish disputes, boys frequently stab each other with knives, two instances of which have occurred since our resi- dence here. No correction was administered in either case, the act being rather looked upon as a promising trait of character . . . [The boys] begin to assert their independence as soon as they can walk, and by the time they reach the age of fourteen, have completely learned the use of the rifle, the arts of trapping beaver and otter, killing the bear, deer and buffalo, and dressing skins and making moccasins and leather clothes. They are then accomplished in all customary things, and are, therefore, capable of supporting themselves and a family.

Ben Ayres could claim no such resume, but he had the good looks and charm to win Fern's heart, and as a young schoolteacher, she may have had enough of rowdy local boys. A month before they were married in 1923, Ben and his friend, who had worked as carpenters, were hired to help a local farmer replace the floor of his cabin. When they removed the old floor, they discovered a Yocum silver dollar. Encouraged by the initial find, the farmer worked with the young men, eagerly dismantling most of the cabin, but only four more Yocum dollars were found there.

The event proved somewhat contagious, apparently, because Artie writes of how his dad caught the bug, and spent most of his time in search of the Lost Silver Mine, rather than on the common pursuits thought necessary to provide for his family. He died a romantic and a dreamer, seven years after his marriage and just four years after Artie was born.

Artie is a bit of his mother, as shown by his industry and flair with a pen. He is equal parts his father, for he has never been able to shake the dream of waking up one day to find the Lost Silver Mine. As a boy riding horseback across unfenced acres to round up his grandparents' cattle, he would stop to poke around and look where a few of those silver dollars might be hidden. As a man, I doubt he ever bought land without wondering if the legendary lode might be hidden there. But his mother's practical side would soon have him focused back on whatever the task was at hand.

In 1958 Joseph Yokum, great grandson of Solomon Yoachum (for a teacher in some classroom had seen fit to change the family name yet again), approached Artie while on a visit from California with a proposal to buy a little farm Artie and his mom had bought together at the junction of Highways 76 and 13. After

Ben died, Fern lost their farm in foreclosure, so the answer, now that she owned property free and clear, was "no." A counter proposal to purchase mineral rights piqued curiosity, but was complicated, so still the answer was "no."

Artie Ayres showed the author the original map, which is too faint and fragile for reproduction. Above is the replica copy Artie paid artist Helen Long to duplicate in careful detail for his book *Traces of Silver*.

A friendship between Joseph Yokum and Artie Ayres developed, and eventually Joseph told Artie the missing details of the Lost Silver Mine legend as he wrote about it in *Traces of Silver*, which I have tried to accurately summarize here. According to Joseph, on his deathbed Sol told the entire story to his grandson, William, and William passed the story on to his son, Joseph, complete with a map. Knowing he was nearing the end of his life, Joseph left the faint penciled map with Artie, saying he hoped if Artie ever put it to good use, he would share the treasure with Joseph. In 1960 a Christmas card to Joseph from Artie was answered with a note that Joseph had died.

Artie dug and reconnoitered. He drilled and reconnoitered again. So far the treasure of the Lost Silver Mine still eludes him, but the rich rewards of searching keep him searching again and again.

Although Ayres's story certainly seems to be a logical possibility, more recent research has uncovered a potential twist to his account. In the Spring 1985 issue of the *White River Valley Historical Quarterly*, Missouri Historian Lynn Morrow offers an interesting alternative theory to the legend of the Lost Silver Mine and the Yocum Silver Dollar. Artie Ayres knows Lynn Morrow well, and is the person who urged this author to read Morrow's writings, even though they cast the legend of the Lost Silver Mine in an entirely different light.

Morrow points out that other legends of Indian silver mines are told about the Buffalo River in Arkansas and the Ouachita Mountains near Hot Springs. One legend tells of silver in "such an abundance that the Indians shod their horses with it." Some would have it that petroglyphs in Ozarks caves are codes that will lead one to treasures of gold or silver. With considerable research to back him up, Morrow makes a reasonable claim that the

> . . . history, tradition, and folklore of the monetary unit designated as a 'dollar' and associated with the family name 'Yocum' span four centuries and perhaps much longer, on at least two continents. In America the legend is connected with the famous 'Mississippi Bubble' land speculation, and its Ozark genesis occurred in the midst of the most significant chapter in the history of Indian migrations in the Missouri and Arkansas Ozarks.

> According to Morrow's thesis, the Delaware received payments in silver, plus their ephemeral land grants in the Ozarks, which placed them in proximity with unscrupulous, exploitive white settlers. John Campbell, the Indian agent for the reservation, complained of many ways in which settlers were disenfranchising the Indians, but most significantly, "Solomon Yoachum has erected a distillery . . . and has made a quantity of peach brandy and has been selling it for some time in quantities to the Indians. There is a number of those outlaw characters all below him who are selling whiskey constantly to the Indians.

With more good scholarship than the average reader wants to search out for himself, Morrow comes to the crucial conclusion,

Ozarkers have continued to believe that the Yoachums produced silver dollars with raw ore taken from 'Silver Cave.' What
seems never to have occurred to the perpetuators of the legend
is that the silver probably had not come from the earth, but
from federal specie given to the Delaware Nation . . . it is clear
that Solomon Yoachum had actually moved onto Indian lands,
raised corn, and made illicit alcohol; furthermore, it is clear . . .
that Campbell forced Yoachum and Denton [another distiller] .
. . to move. Following their eviction from Delaware lands, they
resettled a few miles south . . . and established a series of brandy
and whiskey stills. The Yoachums were after profits, profits from
government annuities sent to the Delawares.

To be caught with silver coinage that could link a person
to illicit trade with the Indians would carry heavy penalties.
Melting silver coins and using them to mint private coinage was,
however, perfectly legal, if one did not consider the source. The
legends of silver mines, which dated all the way back to the time
of DeSoto in the sixteenth century, offered the Yoachums the
perfect cover under which to launder money. Morrow points
out they might have used the ruse to launder silver for other
distillers, as well.

A remote location, sparsely populated by a poorly educated,
superstitious people who were hostile to governmental authority made the White River Valley a perfect place to pull off a
nineteenth-century scam. To make matters better still, Missouri

had no state bank, and the banks that had existed over-printed worthless paper currency, so anyone who had been cheated by the banks was more than willing to accept private silver trade coins from a neighbor, especially if it had a plausible story attached. Considering those circumstances, the Yoachums likely would have been glad to spread rumors of their secret mine.

When the Delaware Nation was moved to land near Kansas City in the mid-1830s, the source of silver would have begun to dry up, and the time to move on to other ventures was nigh. Diversification into land speculation, farming, and milling proved profitable for the family members who remained in the area. It is perfectly plausible none of the younger generations would have known the truth. Supplies of existing Yocum Silver Dollars were then worth much more than their "face" value, so speculators would have eagerly gathered them up and melted them down. Today they would be so rare that, if you could find one still in existence, it would be worth a pretty penny, indeed.

But the stories thus far leave a few unanswered questions.

If there were no mine, there could be no collapse. If there were no collapse, how did Jim and Winonah die? Was it possible her Delaware heritage and loyalty to her people caused some sort of rift between brothers? With a flood of silver beginning to ebb, was mere greed and jealousy cause for a double homicide? But if there were no secret stores of silver remaining, why would Solomon Yoachum, on his deathbed, tell a favorite grandson he should return to find the lost mine? Is it possible there is a cache of silver, buried with two bodies, and the map William gave Joseph, which is now in Artie's possession, might lead there?

Artie hasn't found it. Perhaps he never will. There's a facsimile map in every out-of-print copy of *Traces of Silver* people keep stealing from the libraries. (You'd think nobody knew how to use a copy machine.) Artie may not care. He's sitting on land in Branson West that just keeps getting more and more valuable. If a treasure in silver was ever buried there, chances are, it is buried there still.

CHAPTER 5

A Larger-Than-Life Lady

Ella Kate Ewing had the misfortune to be born in 1872, before medical science could diagnose or treat the condition that would shape her tortured body and legendary life. At the same time, she had the relatively good fortune to be born near the beginning of the Victorian Era's obsessive fascination with everything exotic and bizarre. With profound faith, remarkable grace, and strength of character hard to imagine today, the woman known as the "Missouri Giantess" took control of her destiny and created a vastly better life for herself and her family. She took measure of her small, circumscribed world and adjusted it to fit her needs. As a result, "Miss Ella," as she was known to those who knew and loved her, lived a lifestyle that would have been out of her reach had she been just an ordinary woman in those un-liberated times.

Before her death in 1913, Ella Ewing traveled throughout North America, meeting throngs of people both rich and poor. Colorful posters and glowing publicity announced her arrival

Ella Ewing's mother was above-average height, but her daughter towered over her.

almost everywhere she went. Her name was familiar to most Americans who traveled or read. Although by all accounts shy and demure, she conducted the business of her life without compromise, entertained quite actively at home with her family and friends, and dispensed the kind of charity to others that different individuals in her situation might certainly have needed themselves. All in all, hers was not a bad life for a sideshow freak.

For the ugly word "freak" was the most common name by which people like Ella were usually known in the nineteenth century. Other names frequently used were "weirdo," "monster," "oddball," "eccentric," and "geek." As unimaginably heartless, cruel, and politically incorrect any of those words might seem to us today, during Ella's lifetime they were used without compunction. Few people could have turned a mysterious affliction into an advantage as Miss Ella eventually did.

While Ben and Annie Ewing were still just a young couple living in the Mississippi River town of LaGrange, Missouri, they were blessed with the birth of their first and only child. Before Ella was a year old, the Ewings bought eighty acres of wooded land near the little frontier settlement called Rainbow, outside Gorin, Missouri. From the size of the parcel, it is probable their purchase was one of the many cheap land deals initially made possible by the Homestead Acts. After the Civil War, further encouragement from the federal government was intended to push population expansion westward along proposed railroad routes. A busy and profitable rail line was established through Gorin as settlement began to stretch away from the river routes that had dominated commerce until then, and soon Gorin would become the second-largest city in Scotland County.

But the Ewings remained a poor, struggling farm family. The best land in the burgeoning agricultural region of northern Missouri was bought quickly in large parcels by wealthy settlers from states like Virginia and Kentucky. The Civil War freed their slaves, but their accumulated wealth and resources still gave those people economic advantages. Small landholders, who tended to be the poor migrants from those same wealthy states, European immigrants, or settlers from the less prosperous states like West Virginia and Tennessee, never had slaves and were lucky if their farms were located near the railroad. Ben Ewing's more remote land was not easy for one man to clear, and access to the supplies and markets provided by the railroad were many miles away by slow wagon travel.

Until she was about seven years old, Ella Ewing developed normally. Then suddenly her parents began to notice her hands, feet, arms, and legs were growing unusually fast. According to various accounts, by the time she was twelve years old she was taller than her mother, at 5'6." She was as tall as her 6'2" father when she was just fourteen. By the age of sixteen Ella was nearly 7' tall, and by eighteen years of age she was reportedly 7'8". There appears to have been some exaggeration of her height when she ultimately appeared before the public for pay, with common mentions of her full height given as 8'4". *The Guinness World Records* will not accept any of the sources making such grandiose claims for Ella's height, but numerous photographs appear to give credence to the belief she was nearly 8 feet tall.

Modern medicine recognizes Ella's extremely rare condition as gigantism. The cause is most commonly a benign tumor of the pituitary gland, resulting in excessive production of growth hormone during childhood, adolescence, and beyond. (If a similar disorder of the pituitary gland occurs in later adulthood, the condition is termed "acromegaly," and the individual will not grow as tall, but will suffer with enlarged hands, feet, and face.) Several options including surgery and radiation therapy exist for treatment of gigantism today, but in the nineteenth century the condition was little understood by scientists. No treatment whatsoever was available to slow or stop uncontrolled growth. Less rational minds attributed gigantism to all sorts of fearful imaginings and superstitions.

Ella's less visible symptoms would have included delayed puberty, impaired vision, headaches, excessive sweating, irregular menstrual cycles, spontaneous lactation, general weakness, and fatigue. Ultimately, as an older adult she must have begun to experience the same symptoms of jutting jaw and protruding forehead that persons with acromegaly demonstrate. Because gigantism occurs in childhood, before bone growth plates have closed, the heights untreated individuals can reach cause them to tower over adults long before they are adults themselves. In an unenlightened age, some ignorant people who did not know her doubtlessly jumped to the conclusion Ella was abandoned by God, possessed by the devil, or at very least living in some state of existence that was less than human.

But in her little home community stretching from Rainbow to Gorin, Ella Ewing was loved. She had many friends among the other children, and played with them normally until her rapid growth made her more awkward. Even then, people made accommodations for her, and she enjoyed less-active children's games and typically feminine pursuits like cooking and needlework. Ella, like her parents, was deeply religious, soft spoken, and polite. She had a pleasant demeanor that made her popular with adults. Gradually accustomed to Ella's increasing size, local residents seemed to think little of it.

In adolescence Ella suffered a fall while playing, which her family thought caused her curved spine and slightly stooped posture, but these, too, were probably symptoms of her gigantism. As she continued to grow, she could not walk about her family's home without continually bending over. She could not look out the windows while standing up or comfortably sit in a normal adult chair. Her legs, which were the most outsize part of her body, would not fit under the Ewings' tables. A regular bed would not accommodate her oversize frame. With Ben's meager income, the family could not afford to buy customized furniture, so they improvised as best they could. The amount of material needed to make dresses for Ella meant the family would struggle just to keep her properly clothed as she grew.

One account of Ella Ewing's life was written by area resident Bette Wiley, who claims she is in possession of a diary kept by Annie Ewing from the time Ella was born until Annie died in 1900. Mrs. Wiley declines to show the diary, because she says it contains a mother's innermost thoughts regarding her daughter's difficult life. As a result, it is difficult to determine precisely which accounts described in the book, titled *Our Miss Ella* and now out of print, are direct quotes and which are the author's embellishments. Bette Wiley described her work as follows:

. . . This is not a history book per se', about the families of Miss Ewing or about her friends. It is a projection of the memories left to us by them as human interest experiences, with most of the research material coming from her own Mother's private daily log, a worn and weathered, leather bound tablet in which Annie Ewing wrote daily and, at times, bared her very soul, with intimate and traumatic events and experiences, sometimes very tragic, sometimes delightfully comical. She kept notes in it from the time her child was born until the day of her own death. . . . That same daily log came into my possession during the winter of 1943. My husband Glen brought it home in a box of junk he had bid on and got stuck with at a household auction somewhere in the Gorin area. When I asked my mother-in-law who Annie Ewing was, she told me that she was the mother of that tall girl who had lived south of town a way. The girl's name was Ella. . . . Much of what you will read will be Annie's own words.

In some instances I have taken the liberty to put her thoughts into a more readable form. Dates and names of places are all authentic, as are the names of those people I have mentioned, not for historical purposes but as those who actually did exist and were a part of that particular experience.

A more rigorously researched and authenticated work describing the life of Ella Ewing was written by Barbara Chasteen (now Campbell), as her master's thesis. The book titled *Ella K. Ewing, Missouri Giantess: 1872–1913* was originally printed in a limited edition and is also out of print. Copies are available on display at the Downing House Museum in Memphis, Missouri (which houses an Ella Ewing exhibit) and in the archive files of the Scotland County Memorial Library. (Both facilities house many newspaper articles and photographs pertaining to Ella Ewing in their archives.)

When Barbara Chasteen Campbell wrote her thesis in 1977, she made it a point to interview most of the people still living at the time who had known Ella Ewing. By so doing she heard directly from the Ewing's family friend, Joseph Buford, how traumatized Ella had been at her first public appearance outside her home community when she was just thirteen or fourteen. According to him, Ella was asked to read the Declaration of Independence at a Fourth of July celebration just outside the nearby town of Wyaconda. In the midst of her reading, Ella became so mortified by the stares and reactions of the audience to her size she broke down in tears and a friend had to finish her reading.

Bette Wiley's retelling of the incident is "on the long ride back home to Gorin Ben Ewing exclaimed, 'By golly dang, they ain't never going to get a chance to do that to our Ella again,' Annie wrote in her journal."

Barbara Campbell learned it was when a former Chicago resident who had become a store owner in Wyaconda wrote a friend back home about the giant girl that Ella's fate began to change. The friend back home was museum owner Lewis Epstein, and he made several trips to visit the Ewings and convinced them to allow Ella to appear before the public at his museum for pay. At first the family steadfastly refused.

'For seven years of our lives, we had watched over and nurtured a perfectly normal and physically beautiful extension of ourselves and our union while we toiled and labored daily in order to establish a loving, peaceful, and God fearing home life,' Annie wrote," according to Wiley. "'There wasn't no Mr. Epstein from Chicago going to come here and tell us what we ought to be doing with our daughter when we had already done the very best we knew how to do in our circumstances and we are quite perfectly happy in doing it.'

(Here above is but one example of the difficulty one has interpreting the diary of Annie Ewing, as transmitted by Bette Wiley, when no other access to the journal has been granted by her. If indeed these were Annie's thoughts at the time, would she not have written more accurately how long they had cared for Ella, who was clearly a teenager by then?)

In any event the Ewings finally relented, reportedly with Joseph Buford advising them, "If people are going to gawk, make them pay."

That first, one-month appearance in 1890 earned Ella $1,000, in advance, with both her parents accompanying her to the Windy City. However difficult it must have been to overcome her shyness, the experience went well enough they agreed upon a second, five-month appearance that winter, for which Ella received $5,000. Back home Ella and her parents spoke with enthusiasm about all they had seen and done in Chicago while they were there.

By then Ella was seeing opportunity in her affliction, and she apparently accepted several offers to appear for pay at local fairs near home. By 1893 she was asked to return to Chicago for the World's Columbian Exposition, better known as the Chicago World's Fair. On that occasion she was billed as the "gentle giantess," in obvious observance of her shy, ladylike demeanor. The fair drew an average of forty five thousand visitors a day in the first month alone, with an estimated twenty seven million visitors attending during the entire six-month run.

After the World's Fair, Ella's fame was widespread, and the "Tallest Woman on Earth" could not escape the notice of the Barnum and Bailey Circus. Before she accepted a contract with that organization, however, she appeared in 1894 at the Keosauqua

Fair in Iowa, where people were charged ten cents per person to enter her tent. On one day alone, at that rather parochial event, a newspaper reported two thousand six hundred people paid to see Ella Ewing.

Two brothers who had been neighbors of the Ewing family back then were interviewed in 1986 and reportedly said, "No one envied Miss Ella's fame or money. She had to endure humiliating stage shows. She dreaded the gawkers and mischievous boys who would prick her legs with pins to see if she was standing on stilts."

But difficulties aside, in 1897 Ella entered into an agreement to appear with the Barnum and Bailey "Greatest Show on Earth" Circus for twenty-six weeks, for $125 a week. For the opening week she traveled by train to New York, where the circus was held at Madison Square Garden. Campbell points to an interview Ella gave the *St. Louis Post Dispatch* on June 1, 1897, during her Barnum and Bailey tour, to show how her attitude toward public appearances had changed.

"It was terribly embarrassing to me at first, but I have almost gotten used to it by now and enjoy the traveling and excitement. I spend my vacations at home, and after a week or so I get very lonesome."

Campbell found that Ella turned down an opportunity to appear with the Barnum and Bailey Circus the following year, apparently because it would require travel to Europe, and she feared sea travel. She instead signed a contract to appear with

Buffalo Bill Cody's Wild West Show, but left that tour halfway through, because she and her mother found the people to be coarse and the appearances demeaning. Ella was showing her growing confidence and an ability to insist on having things her way.

With her accumulated wealth, Ella paid off the mortgage on their family farm and purchased land at Gorin where she had a house constructed to her own design. The 10-foot ceilings, nearly 9-foot doorways, and high windows allowed Ella the ability to walk about more normally and look out without stooping. She had furniture custom-made to fit her needs and entertained often. She apparently enjoyed playing Carrom and Parcheesi with family and friends. She owned one of the first telephones in Gorin, and allowed neighbors without telephones to use hers. Barbara Campbell learned in her research Ella helped others with medical expenses and made other generous charitable gifts. Her Christian faith remained strong.

People have noted Ella designed her own dresses, including the gowns she wore while on tour. Her shoes had to be custom-made, and have been reported to extend as large as size twenty-two and twenty-four. The size of her feet apparently embarrassed Ella, because at most shows she requested a cloth border be used to conceal her feet when she entered and exited. (Or might it be that some attempts were made to make her appear closer to the 8'4" height posters proclaimed?) One newspaper account reported that, when asked to show her shoes, Ella replied, "You want too much for your money."

Fairgoers typically paid ten cents just to see Ella in her tent and twenty-five cents to shake her hand. Souvenir postcards of her were sold for ten cents. Barbara Campbell told me she found reports of stunts that occurred wherein Ella would hold up a large-denomination bill to demonstrate no members of her audience could grasp one from her hand. At the Barnum and Bailey Circus she sat in a special chair to watch other performers in view of the general public, but in her tent she normally stood to receive her visitors. Accounts claiming Ella appeared with Tom Thumb are simply wrong; the two were not contemporaries. As Campbell has pointed out, the most famous short person Ella appeared with was Peter the Small from Russia, who appeared with her in the Barnum and Bailey show.

Throughout her career, Ella shunned the word "freak," although it was inevitably used by some. In her research Barbara Campbell found evidence of one fair where Ella was referred to in publicity as a "freak" and so she never returned to that venue. In those days of notorious "yellow journalism," one false newspaper account reported the supposed marriage of Ella to "Edward" (Edouard) Beaupre, a young man nine years her junior from Canada, who also suffered from gigantism, but there is no evidence the two ever met, nor did Ella ever marry.

She once told a reporter for the *New York World,*

Yes, perhaps I have had what the world might call romances: that is, I have had offers of marriages; but I call them business

MYTHS AND MYSTERIES OF MISSOURI

propositions. And that is not my idea of marriage. As for marriage, I believe my views in regard to it are the same as those of any other truly womanly woman. Wife, mother, and housekeeper are the three things woman's being requires to make her life complete . . . But my size will prevent me from marrying.

Ella's mother died of pneumonia in 1900, while on tour with her in Chicago. Ella remained at home for a year, but returned to a busy tour circuit in 1901, traveling across the United States and Canada at fairs. In 1907 she toured for twenty-nine weeks with the Ringling Brothers Circus (which that year acquired the Barnum and Bailey Circus, but the two circuses would not officially merge for several more years). Afterward, Ella's health caused her to limit her travel schedule considerably, until she finally retired due to health problems in 1911.

Ella was diagnosed with tuberculosis and a variety of other illnesses consistent with her gigantism during the last two years of her life. She lived long for a person with her malady, and had the comfort of being with her father at the end. Reports state they together sang her favorite hymn, "Nearer My God to Thee," just before she died on January 10, 1913 (the date on the monument laid over her grave many years later erroneously gives the date as 1912).

Ella had wished to be cremated, to avoid the possibility her grave might be robbed by unscrupulous exhibitors or vandalized by souvenir hunters. Her father could not bear the thought, however, and went against those wishes. He contacted the Gerth Funeral Service in Wyaconda. Frederick Gerth Sr. arrived with his 6' x 2' cooling table, to perform the embalming in the home, as was customary. Because of Ella's size, he had to place one of her oversize dining room chairs at either end of his table, as extensions, to accommodate her body.

Going without sleep for two days, Gerth recommended an oversize, cement-lined steel display vault, which he acquired, along with a hastily made, custom-built casket. Because the large casket would not fit normally into the hearse, Gerth removed the lower half of the front wall of the hearse, so Ella's casket could slide under the driver's seat and the back doors could be closed. This made certain the funeral procession would be dignified, without the embarrassment of the casket falling out in transit over the bumpy, muddy, rutted roads between the home and the cemetery.

An estimated eight hundred to nine hundred people attended Ella's funeral at the Harmony Grove Church. After the ceremony, cement was poured over the vault containing Ella's casket, so her body could never be disturbed. Ella's father died in 1933, and he was laid to rest next to his wife and daughter.

Ella left no will, and little estate, other than her home and possessions. Her father moved from the home before his death, and eventually it fell into disrepair. Vandals and curiosity seekers speeded the deterioration. Efforts to restore the home were discussed, but before anything could be done, the house was destroyed by fire. The Missouri State House Museum and the Downing House Museum each have manikins depicting Ella, the once-famed Missouri Giantess, and the latter museum contains a few of Miss Ella's furnishings and effects. The large monument over Ella's grave at the Harmony Grove Cemetery has never been corrected to show the accurate year of her death. The physical impressions this once larger-than-life lady left on the world have all but disappeared.

But Ella Ewing stands out in history as a woman who rose to make a good life for herself out of adversity. In a world that wanted to see her as freakish and grotesque, she presented herself as a lady with dignity and pride. She showed caring and compassion toward others, while revealing a bit of her own needs for love and understanding. If the community of people who have lived under the cruel stares and ignorant remarks of those who consider themselves "normal" sought an ambassador to the rest of humanity, they could find none better than Ella Ewing, the woman who stood taller than anyone else.

CHAPTER 6

In New Madrid Order the Malt, Not a Shake

If there is another big earthquake in New Madrid during our lifetime anything like the three earthquakes of nearly mythic proportions that occurred there in 1811 and 1812, more than a third of the people in the United States won't need to check their smartphones to know something earth-shattering has occurred. A whole bunch of us won't have any phone service at all. Some people will be lucky to be alive. A few poor souls may envy the dead.

In recorded history there have been very few earthquakes anywhere in the world to rival even one of the three biggest bumps now usually referred to simply as the Great Quakes. Might sound like a cereal, but it ain't. When these crunchy surprises went "Snap! Crackle! POP!" the Earth was swallowing people up along with their houses. Laypeople today disbelieve the eyewitness accounts from that time period as impossible exaggerations. Geologists who study the fault lines realize the most fantastic stories are entirely

Artists attempted to convey the power of the Great Quakes at New Madrid, near the epicenter in 1811.

believable, but they disagree as to when and whether it will happen again. I keep a bag packed.

Even without the earthquakes, 1811 would have been a year of remarkable natural phenomena. For most of the year, the Great Comet of 1811 was visible to the naked eye, peaking in brightness during October. The last time the comet had been witnessed was during the reign of Egyptian Pharaoh Ramses II, 3,065 years before. The comet came to be known in America as "Tecumseh's Comet," for the rebellious Shawnee Indian chief whose name ominously meant "Shooting Star" or "He who walks across the sky." Tecumseh's enormously popular and equally rebellious brother, known as "The Prophet," had predicted a solar eclipse in 1806, and when governor of Indiana William Henry Harrison defiantly challenged him to repeat the feat in 1811, he did so and another eclipse promptly occurred. There are stories The Prophet had contact with a scholarly astronomer from back East before the eclipses occurred; apparently future president Harrison did not. A "black sun" was said by the Indians to predict a war, and the war was launched by Governor Harrison in November. Wars with the Indians and the British would rage until 1813. You could forgive people for thinking the world just might be coming to an end.

Then at about 2:15 a.m. on December 16, 1811, the first earthquake hit. One witness wrote, "The screams of the affrighted inhabitants running to and fro, not knowing where to go, or what to do—the cries of the fowls and beasts of every species—the cracking of trees falling, and the roaring of the Mississippi—the current of which was retrograde for a few minutes, owing as is supposed, to an irruption in its bed—formed a scene truly horrible."

Conservative estimates put that first earthquake at magnitude 7.7 on the Richter scale, and some place it much higher. The epicenter was probably located a little distance from present-day New Madrid, and the effect was devastating and widespread. The upheaval was so violent it created Reelfoot Lake fifteen miles south of New Madrid and drowned the inhabitants of an entire Indian village along the Mississippi. The river amazingly "ran backwards" for several hours, which may have been a tsunami-like event exacerbated by the eruption of groundwater for miles along the shore, which caused a rapid rise of the water level in the riverbed.

The shockwaves from the first earthquake were felt all the way to the East Coast and north to Quebec. Church bells rang in Boston. President James Madison and his wife Dolly felt them in the White House. A foul, sulfurous fog hovered over the ground, probably the result of warm, muddy geysers erupting into the cool night air. The earth heaved in undulating motions for several minutes, causing some people to describe the sight as "like shaking out a bedsheet," or "waves upon the water." The grinding within the Earth's surface made a fearsome thunderous roar and in places emitted seismoluminescent "earthquake lights," not unlike lightning. Soft, alluvial soils liquefied instantaneously, heaving long-buried carbonized wood and petrified tar balls high into the air and raining them down over a wide area. Huge sections of the riverbank caved into the Mississippi, while submerged debris was thrust up to the surface. Mature trees snapped off in the middle of their trunks from the violent shaking. Islands in the river disappeared. The initial slip between plates along the major fault line is estimated to have been 25 to 30 feet at the highest point, with the fault stretching about eighty-seven miles.

A persuasive scientific paper written by Arch Johnston and Eugene Schweig in 1996 summarizes the most informed studies of the Great Quakes (but when you work for the USGS or the University of Memphis, you can't call them things like that). Their analysis includes the incredible conclusion that, "Globally it dominates all other documented earthquakes of stable continental regions . . . and two thirds of all continental crust . . . . [The] largest earthquakes ruptured at least six (and possibly more than seven) intersecting fault segments, one of which broke the surface as a thrust fault that disrupted the bed of the Mississippi River in at least two (and possibly four) places." If events of this magnitude were to strike today with our high population density and complex infrastructure, severe damage would be assured throughout the mid–Mississippi Valley, with inevitable chaos and destruction radiating outward and far beyond, particularly downstream in the Mississippi Basin.

Estimates of white settlers along the Mississippi in that region suggest only about four thousand inhabitants were living there when the Great Quakes hit, with about half of those in and around New Madrid. The major rivers of this country were like highways cutting through the wilderness back then, with little settlements acting like rest areas with services. Native Americans were certainly more numerous, but little understood, uncounted for the most part, and in the prevailing view back East, unworthy of notice except as a potential threat. Sadly, there is virtually no written history of what native peoples experienced to survive the disaster, but we should not assume their burdens were light. They would have found food sources wiped out, shelters in shambles, and loved ones lost. Many stories suggest the local Indians had an oral history of major earthquake events occurring within the memories of their elders, but geologists tell us nobody in their tribes would have ever experienced anything remotely like this.

One of the most miraculous written accounts of the first terrible weeks of the disaster comes from the maiden voyage of the steamship *New Orleans*, the first steamship to ply the waters of the Mississippi. Aboard was the inventor Nicholas J. Roosevelt, who was a great-granduncle of Theodore Roosevelt and an older relation of Franklin and Eleanor, as well. Nicholas collaborated with Robert Fulton and Robert Livingston on the design of the *New Orleans* by making significant contributions to the mechanics of the paddlewheel. He was making the voyage with his pregnant young wife, Lydia, and their two-year-old daughter as the only official passengers to demonstrate the feasibility of steamship river travel. Their voyage from Pittsburgh to New Orleans took them through the destruction that occurred between the time of the first and second major quakes. More than half the damage would occur after they were safely off the river, but they were lucky to survive even that first major earthquake and its aftereffects. Like a ship that puts out to sea during a hurricane, in some ways they were safer on the river with all its perils than on land that was crushing structures and swallowing inhabitants.

The *New Orleans* was built at a cost of $38,000 and launched in Pittsburgh in the latter part of September 1811. She was very high tech in her day. Inventors Fulton, Livingston, and Roosevelt knew she was capable of maintaining a speed of eight to ten miles an hour on the Mississippi, but few on the frontier would believe it. Crews of the barges, flatboats, and keelboats, who were the freight carriers and ferrymen of the day, were almost unanimous in their belief no ship of her size could challenge the Mississippi or Ohio current and navigate upstream. To prove them wrong, Roosevelt had the captain put in at Cincinnati, where he sold tickets for a few lucrative little trips upstream over the next several days. From there the ship continued downstream to Louisville, Kentucky.

At Louisville the voyage was delayed while Lydia gave birth to a son. Further slowing their journey (and perhaps saving their lives), the Falls of Ohio were deemed too shallow for passage, so they remained in Louisville a few weeks longer for the river to rise. When that finally occurred, they navigated the Falls without incident. Near the present-day city of Owensboro, Kentucky, they stopped to get a sizeable load of fuel from a natural outcropping of coal. Such a heavy load would have endangered the ship while passing over the Falls. When they anchored in the lee of an island on the night of December 15, the Roosevelts must have thought their difficulties and delays all lay behind them. But strangely, Tiger, their enormous black New-foundland dog, would not sleep out on the deck as was his habit, but insisted on sleeping fitfully in the cabin with them that night.

The account, published later by Lydia's younger brother (the famous architect) John H. B. Latrobe, makes clear the initial import of the earthquake was slow to dawn on the passengers and crew. They were at that point well over two hundred miles upstream on the Ohio River from the epicenter of the quake.

> The first shock that was observed was felt on board the New Orleans while she lay at anchor after passing the Falls [Louisville, Ky.]. The effect was as though the vessel had been in motion and had suddenly grounded. The cable shook and trembled, and many on board experienced for the moment a nausea resembling sea sickness. It was a little while before they could realize the presence of the dread visitor. It was wholly unex-pected. The shocks succeeded each other during the night. When morning came, the voyage was resumed; and, while under way, the jar of the machinery, the monotonous beating of the wheels and the steady progress of the vessel, prevented the disturbance from being noticed.

Not yet near the greatest devastation caused by the first earthquake, the Roosevelts stopped briefly to visit their friend John James Audubon at Henderson, Kentucky, where they noted every chimney in the village had been obliterated by the quake.

The *New Orleans* passed through Chickasaw Indian territory next, and the native inhabitants were keenly aware something awful was happening. The land along the river was suddenly flooding without rain, as the violent agitation of the earth pushed up groundwater, sometimes in geysers. When the never-before-witnessed steamship approached, announcing its arrival long ahead of time with the drumbeats of its engine, and spewing forth smoke and sparks from its smokestack as it rounded the bends, the Indians assumed this monster machine of the white man must be the cause of their catastrophe.

On one occasion, a large canoe, fully manned, came out of the woods abreast of the steamboat. The Indians, outnumbering the crew of the vessel, paddled after it. There was at once a race, and for a time the contest was equal. The result, however, was what might have been anticipated. Steam had the advantage of endurance; and the Indians with wild shouts, which might have been shouts of defiance, gave up the pursuit, and turned into the forest from whence they had emerged.

Once back in territory occupied by white settlers, the crew found it necessary to replenish their supply of fuel, stopping to cut wood, which didn't burn as hot or last as long as coal. On some of those stops, white settlers met them with dreadful tales of the calamities taking place on land, and hoping for rescue. The small party on board seemed to experience some guilt, but apparently felt they would endanger their own safety by taking on passengers. This dilemma only increased as they neared the epicenter at New Madrid.

> At New Madrid, a great portion of which had been engulphed [sic], as the earth opened in vast chasms and swallowed up houses and their inhabitants, terror stricken people had begged to be taken on board, while others dreading the steamboat, even more than the earthquake, hid themselves as she approached . . . The would-be refugees had no homes to go to; and ample as was the supply of provisions for Mr. Roosevelt and his wife, it would have been altogether insufficient for any large increase of passengers: and as to obtaining provisions on the way, the New Orleans might as well have been upon the open sea. Painful as it was, there was no choice but to turn a deaf ear to the cries of the terrified inhabitants of the doomed town.

Without communication from anyone beyond the severe damage of the earthquake zone, those aboard must have wondered at times if their experience was occurring worldwide. Depression and an eerie hush fell over the *New Orleans* as it continued south.

> One of the peculiar characteristics of the voyage was the silence that prevailed on board. No one seemed disposed to talk; and when there was any conversation, it was carried on in whispers, almost. Tiger, who appeared, alone, to be aware of

the earthquake while the vessel was in motion, prowled about, moaning and growling; and when he came and placed his head on Mrs. Roosevelt's lap, it was a sure sign of a commotion of more than usual violence. Orders were given in low tones; and the usual cheerful "aye, aye, sir," of the sailors, was almost inaudible. Sleeplessness was another characteristic. Sound, continuous sleep, was apparently unknown. Going ashore for wood was the event of each twenty-four hours, and was looked forward to by the crew with satisfaction, notwithstanding the labor that it involved.

This was not a single earthquake followed by a handful of aftershocks over a few days, as we are accustomed to hearing about in the news today, even after a major earthquake event. Following the first big earthquake at New Madrid, and before the second major quake on January 23, more than two thousand tremors, large and small, were noted. On February 7, a third major earthquake struck the region. By March the number of aftershocks that could be felt since the first huge jolt is estimated to have ranged between six and ten thousand. In addition to the three major earthquakes noted during the entire series lasting three months, at least fifteen more were large enough to be felt and recorded somewhere on the East Coast. No one knew if a little tremor would give way to one larger still, or what might come next. Latrobe wrote:

And yet the men, if not sullenly, toiled silently; and if the earth shook, as it often did, while they were at work, the uplifted axe was suspended, or placed quietly on the log, and the men stared at each other until it ceased. Nor was this depression confined to the steamer. Flat boats and barges were passed, whose crews instead of bandying river wit, as they had done when met on the voyage from Pittsburg to Louisville, uttered no word as the New Orleans went by. Before the travelers had been many days on the Mississippi, they fancied, as they looked at each other that they had become haggard. Mrs. Roosevelt [recorded] that she lived in a constant fright, unable to sleep or sew, or read.

Additional encounters with native inhabitants confirmed they thought the steamship was somehow to blame for the disaster.

Sometimes, Indians would join the wood choppers; and occasionally one would be able to converse in English with the men. From these it was learned the steamboat was called the "Penelore," or "fire Canoe," and was supposed to have some affinity with the Comet that had preceded the earthquake, the sparks from the chimney of the boat being likened to the train of the celestial visitant. Again, they would attribute the smoky atmosphere to the steamer, and the rumbling of the earth to the beating of the waters by the fast revolving paddles.

The captain of the *New Orleans*, an experienced pilot on the Mississippi, several times complained he was lost, because familiar landmarks along the river had entirely disappeared. Familiar islands were altered beyond his recognition and new channels had been sliced through forests he had known for years before. Any possibility of return upstream was unthinkable, given the amount of debris that continued to push inexorably on southward with the flood. Their only option was to stay with the flow and avoid dangerous snags. One night, the *New Orleans* was nearly dragged under when the island to which they were moored sank.

. . . when the steamboat rounded to at night . . . it was thought safer to stop at the foot of an island, which might serve as a break water, taking care the trees were far enough from the boat . . . At times severe blows were struck that caused the vessel to tremble through its entire length. Then there would follow a continuous scratching mingled with the gurgling sound of water. Driftwood had caused sounds of the same sort before, and it was thought that driftwood was again busy in producing them. With morning, however, came the true explanation. The island had disappeared; and it was the disintegrated fragments sweeping down the river, that had struck the vessel from time to time and caused the noises . . . At first, it was supposed, that the New Orleans had been borne along by the current: but the pilot pointed to land marks on the banks which proved that it was the island that had disappeared while the steamboat had kept its place. Where the island had been, there was now a broad reach of the river, and when the hawser was cut, for it was found impossible otherwise to free the vessel, the pilot was utterly at a loss which way to steer.

Amid such danger and confusion, the *New Orleans* miraculously made her way south to her namesake city, often using the power of steam to navigate away from tangles of trees caught on bends and in the channel, which would have doomed the vessel had she been caught there. The Roosevelts went on to pursue many other ventures and adventures, but none such as this voyage through an earthquake, which Lydia Roosevelt referred to throughout her life as "one of anxiety and terror."

Fortunately, for those who lost only land, but lived to tell about it, the country was land poor following the Louisiana Purchase, so if you could prove you had owned land before the Great Quakes that was washed away or submerged, Congress had a remedy. Most of the people so materially devastated received land in Arkansas. Georgia McGill, a friend of this author, shared a copy of a deed her husband's family received in a land sale. It reads in part as follows:

Whereas the charity Justice and wisdom of the congress of the United States an act of 2 17 1815, entitled An Act for the relief of the inhabitants of the late county of New Madrid in Missouri Territory who suffered by earthquake, provides that those whose lands have been materially injured by earthquake shall be authorized to locate the like or a greater quantity on any of the public lands of said territory the sale of which is authorized by law.

Nowadays kids would call this a "do over."

Few accounts are as long or descriptive as the book published by Latrobe, but several excerpts from letters and newspapers are both informative and corroborative. An excellent but sobering compendium of attributed eyewitness accounts exists on the Showme .net website, from which I give but a few startling examples:

. . . he soon found the current changed, and the boat hurried up, for about the space of a minute, with the velocity of the swiftest horse; he was obliged to hold his hand to his head to keep his hat on."

. . . the water ran 12 feet perpendicular . . . Another fall was formed about 8 miles below the town, similar to the one above, the roaring of which he could distinctly hear at New Madrid.

The rushing fire and coals through the water produced a wave that carried the water up stream for the distance of several miles. An eye-witness states the flatboat he was on was carried up the river about four miles.

The violent agitation of the ground was such at one time as induced him to hold to a tree to support himself; the earth gave way at the place, and he with the tree sunk down, and he got wounded in the fall. The fissure was so deep as to put it out of his power to get out at that place, he made his way along the fissure until a sloping slide offered him an opportunity of crawling out.

He states that frequent lights appeared—that in one instance, after one of the explosions near where he stood, he approached the hole from which the coal and land had been thrown up, which was now filled with water, and on putting his hand into it he found it was warm.

Even John James Audubon, clear up in Kentucky, had an experience he wrote about later, which would have occurred after he had seen the Roosevelts, because the quake he writes about took place in daylight.

I had proceeded about a mile, when I heard what I imagined to be the distant rumbling of a violent tornado, on which I spurred my steed, with a wish to gallop as fast as possible to the place of shelter; but it would not do, the animal knew better than I what was forthcoming, and, instead of going faster, so nearly stopped, that I remarked he placed one foot after another on the ground with as much precaution as if walking on a smooth sheet of ice. I thought he had suddenly foundered, and, speaking to him, was on the point of dismounting and leading him, when he all of a sudden fell a-groaning piteously, hung his head, spread out his four legs, as if to save himself from falling and stood stock still, continuing to groan.

I had never witnessed any thing of the kind before, although, like every other person, I knew of earthquakes by description. But what is description compared with the reality? Who can tell of the sensations which I experienced when I found myself rocking as it were on my horse, and with him moved to and fro like a child in a cradle, with the most imminent danger around, and expecting the ground every moment to open and present to my eye such an abyss as might engulf myself and all around me. The fearful convulsion, however, lasted only a few minutes, and the heavens again brightened as quickly as they had become obscured; my horse brought his feet to the natural position, raised his head, and galloped off as if loose and frolicking without a rider.

Audubon appears to have gone with the flow as well as anybody, for that eminent observer of every natural wonder soon decided,

Strange to say, I for one became so accustomed to the feeling as rather to enjoy the fears manifested by others. I never can forget the effects of one of the slighter shocks which took place when I was at a friend's house, where I had gone to enjoy the merriment that, in our western country, attends a wedding.

The ceremony being performed, supper over, and the fiddles tuned, dancing became the order of the moment. This was merrily followed up to a late hour, when the party retired to rest. We were in what is called, with great propriety, a Log-house, one of large dimensions, and solidly constructed. The owner was a physician, and in one corner were not only his lancets, tourniquets, amputation-knives, and other sanguinary apparatus, but all the drugs which he employed for the relief of his patients, arranged in jars and phials of different sizes. These had some days before made a narrow escape from destruction, but had been fortunately preserved by closing the doors of the cases in which they were contained.

Every person, old and young, filled with alarm at the creaking of the log-house, and apprehending instant destruction, rushed wildly out to the grass enclosure fronting the building. The full moon was slowly descending from her throne, covered at times by clouds that rolled heavily along, as if to conceal from her view the scenes of terror which prevailed on the earth below.

On the grass-plat we all met, in such condition as rendered it next to impossible to discriminate any of the party, all huddled together in a state of almost perfect nudity. The earth waved like a field of corn before the breeze: the birds left their perches, and flew about not knowing whither; and the Doctor, recollecting the danger to his galipots, ran to his shop-room, to prevent their dancing off the shelves to the floor.

Never for a moment did he think of closing the doors, but spreading his arms, jumped about the front of the cases, pushing back here and there the falling jars; with so little success, however, that before the shock was over, he had lost nearly all he possessed.

The shock at length ceased, and the frightened females, now sensible of their dishabille, fled to their several apartments. The earthquakes produced more serious consequences in other places. Near New Madrid, and for some distance on the

Mississippi, the earth was rent asunder in several places, one or two islands sunk for ever, and the inhabitants fled in dismay towards the eastern shores.

Like Audubon, finding amusement where we can, with his description of what we can infer was "only" a mid-range aftershock, let us leave the "what happened then," and address the "when will it happen again?"

Scientists simply don't know. Most seem to believe as violent a series of events could occur within a thousand years of the last batch. Many experts I read estimate the "interval" could be upwards of a mere four hundred to six hundred years. Two hundred years have already gone by, remember. How much do you trust the weatherman?

Whereas we say there were four thousand people plus Indians, in the old math way of counting such things, today we know there are millions of inhabitants all over the primary at-risk zones of the Great Quakes. Think tall buildings, structurally weak homes, natural gas pipelines, high-tension wires, nuclear power plants, hydroelectric dams, toxic wastes, bridges . . . need I go on? If we ever have to live through a series of earthquakes as violent as those Audubon survived and lived to laugh about, I just hope we can find at least one good thing to laugh about before the day we die.

Or as my friend Felder Rushing, the crazy garden guru from Mississippi, loves to say of any contemplated catastrophe, "You may only have time to say, 'Oh, no!' or 'Eee-hah!' and I'd rather die saying 'Eee-hah!'"

CHAPTER 7

Tom Bass: Legendary Horse Whisperer

A great mystery of this world is why the name of Tom Bass is so little known today. His achievements in the realm of horse training and equestrian arts might be disbelieved in our car-crazy world, had not so many famous and respected individuals witnessed and testified to them as they occurred. Nevertheless, Tom Bass's achievements are nothing short of legendary—he truly was the horse whisperer of his day. He could take a violent, angry horse sentenced to slaughter and train the animal to accept a saddle and rider without ever using a whip. More than any other man, he changed the way horses were treated all over the world.

That alone would make him worthy of his legend, but with the same air of confidence and dignity with which he won so many horse shows, Tom Bass greatly advanced the position of racial minorities in America after the Civil War. Never violent or confrontational with either horses or men, Tom Bass was the first to cross numerous color barriers in America, which he accomplished merely by being himself.

Tom Bass was born a slave near Columbia, Missouri, on January 5, 1859. His mother was the slave Cornelia Gray; his father, her master, was William Hayden Bass, son of the wealthy plantation owner Eli Bass. As was common in that time and place, Tom's father never denied his slave son's paternity, but neither did he grant him status above any other slave. While Cornelia was pregnant with Tom, William Hayden Bass married his fiancée, Irene Hickman. Cornelia then became Irene's lady's maid. Cornelia had no other children by William; Irene bore William one daughter and seven sons. As a young child, Tom remained a slave until he was freed by the Emancipation Proclamation.

The Civil War upset the fortunes of a great many white men and women in Little Dixie, as that part of north central Missouri was known back then. Eli Bass saw his slaves freed against his will, lost a considerable part of his wealth and died, some say, a broken man. By all accounts, William Hayden Bass managed his share of what was left of the family property well and moved into business ventures in the city of Columbia, where he continued to prosper. Once freed, Cornelia sought employment in Columbia, but Tom and his maternal grandparents who raised him continued to work after the Civil War on another Bass family estate. Tom's maternal grandfather, Presley Gray, had been freed before the war, and appears to have enjoyed more than a little respect in the community. Tom often cited advice his grandfather gave him, when sharing his own modestly expressed sensible opinions on both horses and men.

THE STATE HISTORICAL SOCIETY OF MISSOURI

Tom Bass and Belle Beach are said to be the best pairing ever of a High School–style horse and rider.

Passenger automobiles were just the foolish fantasy of dreamers in those days. Vehicular highway transportation was by wagons, coaches, carts, and carriages. Models of carriages were almost as varied and numerous as those automobile manufacturers create today, with names like "Gigs," "Spiders," "Wagonettes," "Phaetons," "Breaks," "Broughams," "Victorias," and "Landaus." (When you look over the list, it appears we haven't made such great progress naming our vehicles in the last hundred years.)

Some of those fancy little horse-drawn carriages could zip around almost like chariots, but the real roadsters, sport racers, off-road conveyances, and ATVs of the day were the American Saddlebred horses developed steadily in the United States beginning about the time of the American Revolution. In the same way America would later dominate the automobile industry, the country dominated the equestrian world almost from the birth of our nation. Americans looked back across the Atlantic for the traditions and culture of horse showmanship, but Europeans and people the world over made pilgrimages to America for the very best horse-flesh. Tom Bass turned the attention of equestrians worldwide to the show arenas in Missouri with his unparalleled mastery of horse training. Not only were American steeds strong and sleek; thanks to training methods introduced by Tom Bass, those magnificent animals were well-tuned to a rider's commands, as well.

The story of Tom's first remarkable feat as a horse trainer occurred when the boy was just nine years old. It also demonstrates his ability to rise above the routine petty racism that was all too common following the Civil War. Little Tom had been riding since he was "no bigger than a horsefly," as he liked to say. Humorous hyperboles aside, there are several believable accounts of how Tom, when just a toddler, would walk confidently under the bellies of horses so tall, he didn't even have to stoop. It is accepted fact he was allowed to ride horses alone when he was just four years old. By the age of six he was jumping fences. At seven Tom was given a balky old mule by his grandfather. Mr. Potts, as the mule was called, would not plow or pull a wagon. He wouldn't tolerate a lead and he refused to be ridden. If Tom had not accepted the challenge of training Mr. Potts, the stubborn old creature would doubtless have been sold to a mule skinner.

One day one of Tom's half-brothers and two of his school friends were awkwardly trying to ride some of the family's good horses in the arena near the stables. The white boys noticed Tom watching with what they deemed to be disrespect. The boys arrogantly shouted racial slurs and indignities at Tom, taunting him with insults and insinuations that he would do far worse, if he were even allowed to ride one of the prize mounts.

Tom ran off, but not to surrender. Minutes later he reappeared, wearing his grandfather's oversize white shirt and large black coat. He was riding Mr. Potts. The commotion drew his father, just in time to see Tom put on a show for the boys with Mr. Potts. With Tom in the saddle and holding the reins, the outlaw mule cantered around the arena and performed the five basic movements of modern dressage. As an amazing finale, Tom caused Mr. Potts to canter backward around the arena, which no horse had ever been known to do. William Bass chided the white boys, saying they would do well to observe young Tom and learn from his skill as a horseman. The story went quickly around, from stables to studies, that there was a little black boy in Boone County who could work miracles with a horse or a mule.

Such actions don't endear little boys to each other, so Tom's life on the Bass plantation could not have gotten much easier as a result. Soon after, Tom got his first real job at a hotel in Columbia, beginning modestly by transporting customers in a buggy between the railroad station and the hotel. He "graduated" to also serve as a bellhop for a while, but as his reputation as a horse trainer spread, he began making money by helping train the mounts of local townspeople.

Next, a very different Mr. Potts helped advance the career of Tom Bass when the young man was just twenty years old. Joseph Potts, of Mexico, Missouri, in nearby Audrain County hired Tom to work as a horse trainer. Potts was a respected trainer, himself, and owner of Thornton Star, a prized stallion regarded as one of the founders in the American Saddlebred horse line. Joseph Potts's business partner, Cyrus Clark, voiced strong objections, expressing fears their white clientele would go elsewhere when they learned Potts had hired a black man to train their horses. Potts would have none of it, however, being one of the first white men to vouch for the character of Tom Bass and claiming him to be an extraordinary judge of horseflesh.

Each year Potts and Clark would stage a small show and sell their current crop of saddle-trained horses. One season, not long after Tom was hired, the partners found they were still short of enough stock to make a good showing to the public. At the last minute Tom came forth with half a dozen horses he had acquired as "unfit to ride," which he demonstrated could now be ridden by even a delicate lady. The sale was a success and Clark grudgingly admitted Tom Bass was a remarkable horseman.

About the same time Tom invented a more humane bit, which transformed the way horses were trained and ridden forever.

Previous bits were short and cut deeply into the horse's mouth, on the theory a bit should be used to painfully command the animal's attention. The Tom Bass bit was heavier, featuring a longer shank and a higher port, in order to just lightly touch the roof of the horse's mouth. Potts immediately saw the wisdom of the change and urged Tom to patent his invention. Tom feared a patent might slow the new bit's acceptance, and thus mean more horses would be tortured by the cruel bits of the day. Without patent restrictions, the new bit and slight variations of the design proliferated, with the result that horses benefitted, but Tom Bass did not become rich from his revolutionary invention. He always claimed he slept better at night knowing so many horses had been spared the cruel treatment of the old ways.

While still in the employ of Potts and Clark, Tom took on the challenge of training a man-killing mare known as "The Blazing Black." Although a beautiful horse, the mare would scream, kick, and bite at anyone who approached her. When she was moved, it took groups of men who would arm themselves with pitchforks to get her in or out of her stall. Over time Tom patiently taught her to accept his presence, receive his touch, take a bit, go on lead, and finally let him saddle her. It took weeks of more patient training before Tom felt she was ready to accept his weight in the saddle. Ultimately, he taught The Blazing Black to perform as well as any of the finest show horses in the country, but she would only allow Tom Bass to ride her. When a man who was terrified to work around the mare expressed amazement Tom had not been killed, Tom replied, "If she had wanted to kill me, she would have let me know."

A day came when Potts and Clark had no entry in the four-year-old category of a very prestigious horse show. A win at such an event would drive a good deal of business their way. No black man had ever competed against white gentry at a major horse show. Riding show-quality horses was a sport to which even a lower-class white man need not apply. Everyone was stunned when Joseph Potts entered Tom Bass riding The Blazing Black. Perhaps because no such thing had ever occurred, and no advance notice was given, there was no formal protest. Spectators were in awe to see the killer mare perform flawlessly for Tom, and he placed second for a red ribbon. Potts was furious Tom and The Blazing Black had not taken the blue ribbon, because it was apparent to everyone which horse and rider had truly won. Tom knew the victory was in the fact he had been allowed to compete at all. He said he remembered being told by his grandfather Presley Gray to be fearless in his conduct, because "our people need your success."

Joseph Potts retired in 1883. Tom took his advice and started his own horse-training stable on a few rough acres out on the edge of town. He had married Mexico's first black school teacher, Angie Jewell, the year before, and he was eager to provide a good home for her. Without the means to clear his land, Tom persuaded a local contractor to do the job in exchange for Tom's training his high-spirited team of horses to get over their debilitating fear of trains. Tom did so by blindfolding the pair, loading them on a train car, and taking them to the stockyards in Kansas City, where he soothed them all night while they listened to the melee of train traffic in the busy yard. When Tom returned to Mexico with the team, they no longer bolted at the sound of an oncoming train.

Joseph Potts had prospered with horses like Thornton Star and The Blazing Black in his stable. Now Tom needed a great horse to demonstrate his skills. Such horses were commonly called "brag horses" in the trade, but former slave Tom Bass was not likely to brag and risk being labeled "uppity." More than any other horse trainer, Tom needed a horse that would proclaim his competency for him. One day he came home leading a leggy gray colt he had spotted among a herd of cattle and purchased on the spot for $100. He told Angie he had named the colt Columbus, because "Columbus discovered America, and I discovered Columbus."

Even as a colt, Columbus responded to voice commands and showed a fearless temperament. Tom said the young horse could open almost any gate with his teeth, and if a gate wouldn't yield, he would crawl under the fence constraining him. Tom, who was acquainted with many world-class horses by then, said he never knew of a smarter horse. After years of careful training, Tom Bass and Columbus were ready for their first big show.

For the gelding's debut Tom chose the prestigious St. Louis horse show. Many famous equestrians had ridden in the St. Louis event, including General Ulysses S. Grant before he became president. Never before had a black man been allowed to show there, but Tom Bass was rapidly becoming a legend. With firm resolve Tom entered Columbus in the High School competition, which was considered the most difficult class. The rules required horse and rider to perform a series of difficult maneuvers to music. With his trusted master astride him, Columbus racked, leaped, pirouetted, and pranced. Spectators who witnessed the performance described the pair as looking like a centaur, rather than two separate beings. As a finale, Tom coaxed Columbus to canter backward around the arena, turn around completely on his hind legs "like a ballerina," then kneel on one leg and bow before the startled judges. Shaking his head in amazement, one of the judges was heard to say he would have thought the display was "an impossible feat for horse or horseman."

If Tom had been a local legend in Little Dixie, just along the Missouri River, his performance with Columbus at the St. Louis horse show proved to spectators from all across the country the legend was true. As word spread, the famous showman Buffalo Bill Cody appeared on Tom Bass's doorstep with an offer to buy Columbus "at any price" to be his personal mount in his famed Wild West Show. Tom was said to have valued Columbus more like a child than a mere horse, but like a proud parent, he saw the opportunities for Columbus to go beyond his world in Missouri and thrive on the attention of crowds he enjoyed. Above all, Buffalo Bill Cody was reputed to be a lover of horses, so Tom knew Columbus would be treated well. A fair deal for the horse was struck and the men became lifelong friends.

Tom traveled to Chicago and won the Columbian Exposition horse show in 1893, but racism persisted. One bitter white competitor who had lost to Tom in the arena pointedly asked him if the "Bass bit" was named for his father. One year he was not allowed to ride in the Iowa State Fair horse show in Des Moines, after he journeyed there to compete with several mounts. When his white friends from Mexico heard of the slight, they insisted he remain and allow them to ride his horses for him, and in that manner, they took most of the ribbons on his behalf. The following year pressure was put on the organizers to allow Tom to ride, and he, with his horses, swept almost every category.

In 1902 tragedy struck when Buffalo Bill returned to Mexico and invited Tom to ride Columbus in a demonstration. Executing a particularly difficult maneuver, Columbus fell backward and landed on his former master, crushing Tom's pelvis and nearly killing him. Witnesses described how Columbus got back up in great distress, pawing at the ground and attempting to lift the injured rider with his teeth by his clothing. When word of the accident reached London, writers for the *Times* wired the newspaper in little Mexico, Missouri, and asked to be updated as to Tom's condition. At first it appeared the great horseman might never ride again, but after more than a year of painful recovery, he resumed riding and training horses.

Two years after his accident, Tom attempted to buy a foal he thought had great potential. Her owner was his former employer, Cyrus Clark. Joseph Potts had died, and Clark had no compunction in continually raising the price of the foal until she was out of Tom's reach. At the age of three the filly ultimately sold at a ridiculously high price to a military man as a buggy horse for his wife. Within a few months and without sufficient training, the high-spirited horse threw her mistress through a plate glass window, at which point the army captain sold Belle Beach to Tom Bass. The pairing was to be one of the greatest matches in equestrian history.

Belle Beach was said to be perhaps the fastest-gaited mare ever seen in Missouri. She performed all the difficult maneuvers of High School competition, plus the legendary Tom Bass backward canter and the turn on hind legs with forelegs extended that had proved nearly fatal for Tom Bass with Columbus. In a highly unusual bit of showmanship, Tom dismounted and faced Belle Beach, at which point she waltzed with him to the tune of "After the Ball Is Over" and danced a jig when the music changed to "Turkey in the Straw." After that, her graceful kneeling before the judges was almost anticlimactic.

A delegation from France came to Missouri to see for themselves whether the legendary feats of this horse and rider could possibly be true. After a demonstration one of their members declared, "Monsieur Bass, we came to see a horse perform, but what we have witnessed is a wave upon the water."

Tom was invited to bring the horses of his choice to perform at the Diamond Jubilee for Queen Victoria, but he was uneasy at the thought of sea travel, so he regretfully declined, stating neither he nor his horses were good sailors. Another time he said he didn't want to venture so far from land he couldn't spot an oak tree.

Tom Bass did favor Queen Marie of Romania with a command performance while she was traveling stateside. Among the great and famous men who sought out Tom Bass and proudly called him friend were presidents William McKinley, Theodore Roosevelt, William Howard Taft, and Calvin Coolidge. William Jennings Bryan visited, admiring a particularly fine horse, even when he learned the horse's name was William McKinley. Buffalo Bill Cody returned several times, at least one time in the company of a young Oklahoma cowboy by the name of Will Rogers.

In his later years Tom continued to train and ride famous horses that he did not own, including Miss Rex and Rex McDonald (the all-time champion Saddlebred horse). He gave a horse show to raise money for a group to start the first horse show in Kansas City as part of an ongoing livestock event, and so is credited with being a founder of the American Royal. He endured the tragic death of a beloved son and news that Columbus had perished in a horrible stable fire. When the showmen who had so carelessly allowed Columbus to die attempted to purchase another famous horse from Tom "at any price," he continually refused, selling the horse instead to a doctor for several thousand dollars less than he had been offered by the careless show owners.

In 1934 the great showman, humorist, and country philosopher Will Rogers devoted his entire newspaper column to Tom Bass when he died. In a world already obsessed with automobiles, memories of Tom Bass were fading. Will Rogers reminded them of what had been lost with the words:

> Tom Bass, well known Negro horseman, aged 73, died today. Don't mean much to you, does it? You have all seen society folks perform on a beautiful 3-gaited or 5-gaited saddle horse, and said: 'My, what skill and patience they must have to train that animal.' Well, all they did was ride it. All this Negro, Tom Bass, did was to train it. For over 50 years, America's premier trainer, he trained thousands that others were applauded on. A remarkable man, a remarkable character. Many Negroes have been great horsemen; every stable has its traditional stories of what its Negro rider used to do. If old St. Peter is wise as we give him credit for being, Tom, he will let you go in on horseback and give those folks up there a great show and you'll get the blue ribbon yourself.

Tom Bass would summarize his horse-training methods simply by saying, "Horses are like humans." Living through a time when examples of inhumanity toward man and beast were all too common, his actions expressed the conviction redemption is always possible. In a realm dominated by wealth and privilege, this modest man excelled without the benefits of formal education or patrimony. His legacy includes significant improvements in the way horses were treated, and substantial reappraisals of how blacks in America were viewed.

The best place to relive the legendary life of Tom Bass is at the American Saddlebred Horse Museum in Mexico, Missouri. Whether you are a lover of horses or maybe just someone interested in the accomplishments of legendary Americans, you'll be in awe of the achievements of the great horse whisperer of his day. While you are there, whisper a little hello and thank you to old Tom Bass

CHAPTER 8

Mastodons and Mammoths in Missouri

S t. Louis is a large, sprawling American city, filled with the usual complement of residences, highways, shopping malls, gas stations, and grocery stores. You never have to go very far if you want to grab something to eat.

Imperial, Missouri, the nearest town to the Kimmswick Bone Bed and its associated Mastodon State Historic Site, is part of the greater St. Louis metropolitan area. Back in the old days, when folks in those parts were hungry and wanted to grab something to eat, they would head on over to the Kimmswick Mineral Swamp and Salt Lick and grab a mastodon. Of course, we are talking about a time, over ten thousand years ago, when appetites and the rules of etiquette were somewhat different than they are today. As far as we can tell, people back then didn't use paper napkins and they probably never heard of the spork. What they did do was come here, where many animals were drawn to the mineral-rich springs, and use the geologic features of water holes and wallows to help them with their hunts.

I have met uneducated people who think mastodons and woolly mammoths went out with the dinosaurs. Others think there were never animals in North America larger than today's grizzly bears and bison. So what were these beasts that once roamed around here, where today we go to shop and drop the kids off at daycare? What caused their extinction if they were so big and strong? Could any of my relatives be responsible for their disappearance? If someone brings them back, like they say they might, will they be really, really mad at us?

Although these questions remain essentially unanswered after more than two centuries of discovery, exploration, and research, scientists and others continue to preserve what evidence remains and use that evidence to piece together this mysterious puzzle. The Mastodon State Historic Site is a good example of how citizen participation and activism can lead to very important changes, with benefits not fully appreciated at the time. Back about 1970 a group of citizens in and around Jefferson County became concerned an important historic landmark was being lost. Relic hunters had, since the earliest settlement days in the early 1800s, gradually dug and dispersed or destroyed the skeletons of an estimated sixty mastodons, along with other fossils and important remnants of prehistoric eras. Without saving some of this fossil record, our understanding and appreciation of this land we live on would be sadly lacking.

In 1839 the first systematic excavations of this site were conducted by Albert C. Koch, a self-taught paleontologist, entrepreneur, and St. Louis museum owner who extracted huge weathered bones from a mill site on Rock Creek, where they had been discovered in a partially exposed state. Convinced he had discovered a new prehistoric creature, Koch misassembled the skeleton and named it the Missouri Leviathan, or Missourium. He exhibited his skeleton with considerable financial success, but was eventually convinced by a scientist at the British Museum that his find was just a plain old Mastodon americanum, or American mastodon.

At the dawn of the twentieth century, amateur paleontologist C. W. Beehler from St. Louis excavated more impressive fossils and exhibited them in a rustic "wooden shack" museum close to the site. Interest in the site was particularly intense during and after the 1904 St. Louis World's Fair, but Beehler's digs were not well documented, even for that time, so his suggestions of humans in America interacting with animals from the Pleistocene were not taken seriously by the scientific community.

Still more fossil searches in the area were conducted from 1940 to 1942 by Robert McCormick Adams of the St. Louis Academy of Science, but he found few human artifacts with the fossils he recovered, and no further inferences of human/mastodon interaction were made at the time. Later, private digs uncovered an unknown number of fossils and artifacts that were unfortunately unrecorded and widely dispersed to relic hunters and curiosity seekers. Limestone quarrying activity in the area further disrupted the site and rendered some of the potential excavation areas within the site of little value to science today.

Enter the Mastodon Park Committee, a small group of concerned citizens, legislators, and schoolchildren, with corporate support, spearheaded by four people who have been referred to as "particularly determined women." Judging from their success, anyone would want those gals on their team. In 1976 the group, with the help of a federal grant, enabled the Missouri Department of Natural Resources to purchase more than four hundred acres, including the Bone Bed, for a state park now designated a state historic site. The designation is significant, because to qualify as a "historic site" a location must contain evidence of a "milestone of human events," which puts this up there with the era of Missouri's extensive mound-building civilization, European explorations, immigrations, Civil War strife, and the Industrial Revolution in America. Why all the fuss over a bunch of old bones and some arrowheads?

To say the group was "spearheaded" by four women seems particularly apt, because in 1979 a dig at the Kimmswick Bone Bed led by paleontologist Russell W. Graham from Illinois State Museum, using modern techniques of excavation, was able to definitively demonstrate the coexistence of Clovis people (prehistoric hunters known for making stone tools) with mastodons in America. Clovis spear points and other tools associated with butchering large game found in association with mastodon bones gained wide acceptance for the theory, previously put forth, that humans had hunted mastodons and woolly mammoths in North America, thus probably hastening their extinction. Here was proof of mastodon hunting; evidence of the hunting of woolly mammoths would soon be found farther north in Wisconsin and out West. But officials with the Mastodon Historic Site have written of the critical Missouri dig, "This was the first time archaeologists had found evidence of human weapons interspersed with the bones of these giant prehistoric beasts."

That last statement claiming primacy for the Mastodon Historic Site is perhaps not now technically true, because an extraordinary mastodon skeleton was found in 1977 by farmer Emanuel Manis on his property near Sequim, Washington. Excavated almost immediately by archaeologist Carl Gustafson, the skeleton included a rib that had been injured by a pointed object Gustafson declared to be a spear point. Further study of the rib indicated the animal had not died at the time of the injury from the sharp-pointed object, because subsequent bone growth had taken place.

[Note to self: Do not attack a mastodon with a sharp object, unless you intend to finish the job. Chances are you cannot obtain enough meat for even a small sandwich unless the mastodon is dead, and mastodons find deep puncture wounds extremely upsetting.]

Carl Gustafson was spot on when he declared at the time that the object was most certainly a spear point and by his estimate the skeleton was approximately fourteen thousand years old. Nevertheless, a howling over this pronouncement went up in the scientific community that would have made you think someone was trying to kill another mastodon that very day. It took more than twenty years, but in 2011 the journal *Science* came out with an article detailing a reexamination of the skeleton by Professor Michael Waters of Texas A & M University. Using what has been called an "industrial grade" CT (computerized tomography) scanner, many times more powerful than what a doctor uses on you in the hospital, Waters studied slices every 0.06 millimeters throughout (that is about half the thickness of a sheet of ordinary paper), determining, "The 3D rendering clearly showed that the object was sharpened to a tip. It was clearly the end of a bone projectile point."

Waters's examination also included state-of-the-art analysis of collagen proteins from both ribs and tusks of the animal, which gave a confirmed date of death approximately 13,800 years ago. Both spear point and rib were determined by Waters to be comprised of mastodon bone, indicating the beast was attacked with tools made from its own species. A few holdouts have tried to come up with scenarios by which mastodons fighting, or a mastodon rolling onto broken bones might cause such an injury, but the angle of thrust, the depth of the injury, and the apparent sharpening of the tool, convince most of the scientific community otherwise. One disbeliever suggested he would only accept the spear theory if someone would "yank out" the piece of bone and show it to him, which left Waters seemingly aghast, saying he would not commit such a ruinous examination on an iconic find, and if someone wanted more proof, perhaps he would re-create the specimen "with a 3D printer" and the doubting Thomas could yank on that.

Michael Waters, to whom many obviously look now for wise analysis of the fossil record with regard to mastodon extinctions, suggests there was not a "Clovis blitzkrieg" to eliminate mastodons and their mammoth cousins when humans entered North America. Rather he and like-minded colleagues suggest the mammoth and mastodons' extinction would have been gradual, the result of the combined forces of climate change, food shortages, human predation, and even possibly the inadvertent introduction of tuberculosis by humans when they entered the continent across the Bering land bridge.

Back in Missouri, folks at the Mastodon Historic Site don't seem a bit disturbed that the Sequim site find might predate their no-less-significant Missouri find of Clovis tools in association with mastodon bones by a couple of years or less. And what's a couple of years to a hairy elephant that went extinct over ten thousand years ago, anyway? The larger questions almost everyone wants to focus on now are, how far back in time were humans in North America feasting on mammals of the order Proboscidea? and when did they dine on the very last one?

First, it helps to describe the differences between mastodons and mammoths, the only two Elephantiformes humans have ever encountered in North America, outside of a zoo. Mastodons are the little guys, only four to six tons, generally, 8 to 10 feet tall at the shoulders, with 5 foot-long tusks. They appeared first sometime in the late Miocene or Pliocene, way before your grandmother's time, then disappeared probably between ten thousand to eleven

Don't say you're livin' Paleo, dude, until you've killed one of these critters and picked its bones clean.

thousand years ago. Mammoths, in contrast, grew up to weigh ten tons or more, were sometimes 14 feet tall at their shoulders, and had amazing curled tusks that could grow 16 feet long. Unlike the made-in-America mastodons, mammoths ranged over most of the world, but with our North American "Columbia Mammoth" growing the biggest, making it just possibly the largest land mammal to have ever lived.

Whereas mastodons were indigenous to the Americas, mammoths came across the Bering land bridge, along with most early humans. No predators in North America at that time would have posed a threat to an adult mammoth or mastodon, but sick, injured, or young animals of either species would have been likely prey for saber-tooth cats, dire wolves, short-faced bears, and American cave lions. Mammoths appear to have been herd animals with behaviors much like their distant cousins the African elephants. Mass die-offs of groups of mammoths have been found (the evident victims of fires and floods) and analysis of their remains seems to indicate mature females herded with calves and young juveniles, while young males were solitary or loosely grouped together. Mastodons appear from fossil evidence to have been more solitary in their habits.

The disposition of bones in excavation sites can be quite poignant. Even thousands of years later, a good paleontologist can reconstruct an animal's final days and hours, stuck in quicksand or a water hole, pawing to get out. The images scientists describe can be so vivid as to make you think you can hear the echoes of their loud bellows and last breaths. At some sites, calf skeletons have been found in the tusks of their herd mothers, as if, as their final act, these giants attempted to raise their young out of danger. At other sites the bones show signs of having been separated in a butchering process, with marks left by stone tools.

Both mammoths and mastodons were hairy, but mammoths were probably the champions of surviving the cold, hence the name "woolly mammoth," which is so often applied to them. Mastodons were browsers, named for their "nipple-shaped" teeth, which have been described as looking like "bricks with cone-shaped cleats" on them. As browsers, they feasted primarily on tree branches and shrubs, but probably were able to forage on grasses when times got hard. Mammoths were grazing animals whose large adults, each about the size of a school bus, needed about four hundred pounds of food each day. The derivation of the name "mammoth" is a little more in dispute, with meanings said to range from "earth horn" to "earth burrower." It has been said farmers in Northern Eurasia, encountering mammoth bones in their fields, thought they belonged to large creatures that dug tunnels underground.

The first mastodon fossil recognized in America was found in 1705 by a Dutch tenant farmer in the Hudson River Valley. Weighing about five pounds, it was classically shaped like a brick with little cones on one surface. The farmer traded the tooth to a local politician for a glass of rum, and the politician subsequently traded the tooth to Lord Cornbury, then governor of New York.

Lord Cornbury will forever be best known for dressing up as his cousin, Queen Anne, even for public functions, but he did manage to send her the enormous tooth. Getting the tooth to England was probably the best thing Lord Cornbury ever did, because the evidence of the "tooth of a giant" from America was said to give proof of the biblical pronouncement there were giants on Earth before the Flood. Talk of the amazing creature from America, named an "incognitum," or unknown creature, gave greater reputation to the natural wonders of the New World. And any time spent talking about the natural wonders of the New World was time not spent talking about Lord Cornbury and his wardrobe.

Like the indigenous four-legged predators of North America, early Americans would not have engaged a healthy adult mastodon or mammoth on equal footing. Using superior intelligence and cooperative hunting techniques, they are thought to have driven the animals (probably with noise as well as projectiles and fire) into pits and swampy areas around salt licks and mineral springs, where the compromised beasts could be attacked and overwhelmed by many hunters attacking from all sides.

The Kimmswick area of Missouri, with its salty mineral springs, would have been an ideal hunting ground. Somewhat surprisingly, no evidence has been found of highly populated or continuous habitation in the immediate area by humans. It seems probable continual human habitation would have frightened away the beasts, so seasonal or migratory hunts must have proven more effective. Mastodons were apparently relatively numerous in the

Kimmswick area during this period; meanwhile, fossil remains of mammoths have only been found in the north and northwestern portions of Missouri. It is likely mammoths remained in the high plains of what are now the western and southwestern plains of the United States and Canada. Evidence supports that both mammoths and mastodons were equally hunted in those regions.

With each find telling paleontologists more and more, we now also know it was not just the Clovis people who killed and ate the big hairy beasts. Since evidence of Clovis predation of mammoths and mastodons was established, other sites around North America have produced convincing proof of pre-Clovis hunting of these animals, as well.

Probably climate change, plus a sudden influx of other herbivores entering the continent across the Bering land bridge, and humans rapidly altering the environment with fire and cooperative hunting techniques, all combined to seal the fate of large animals like the mammoth and mastodon. Examination of mammoths and mastodons in permafrost reveals the animals were susceptible to tuberculosis, as are modern elephants. DNA and other evidence can demonstrate the bacteria entered North America with the immigration of peoples from Siberia. Subsequent digs may advance the dates of the last certain known kills by humans of mammoths and mastodons in North America, but at present we can estimate it occurred probably a little more than ten tousand years ago.

How excited the last tribe must have been to encounter the last huge beast, mired in the swamp, and knowing they soon would eat well for days. Did one unlucky hunter die or suffer a crippling injury as the animal thrashed about, attempting to protect itself or a calf? Was the kill celebrated with a ritual, hoping to produce other, epic prey, or did they have a sense they might never see its kind again?

As a potential antidote to the unsolved mysteries of these long-gone creatures, science now presents us with the option of "de-extinction," as it has been optimistically termed. Although still in its infancy, reproductive physiologists are experimenting with processes by which complete embryos or other genetic material from extinct creatures can be implanted into related species in hopes of producing viable offspring. In cases where no complete DNA exists from a single individual, researchers theorize it might be possible to gradually, over time, replace portions of DNA sequences from other long-dead members of a species in subsequent generations of partial clones, and in that way gradually "build" a complete specimen capable of reestablishing the breed.

In the case of the mammoth and mastodon, creatures are found with some frequency in the permafrost, where their nearly intact DNA has been surprisingly well preserved. By implanting genes from these long-dead creatures into modern elephant stem cells, some researchers are confident they can eventually bring a healthy mammoth infant to term inside an elephant's womb.

A refuge was created in northeastern Siberia at the end of the twentieth century, where large herbivores such as bison and horses, which are suited to that climate, are being allowed to run wild in an effort to restore the healthy balance necessary to restore grasslands that once dominated the ecosystem. Scientists who favor de-extinction imagine such a place as the perfect setting to reintroduce creatures like mammoths and mastodons. Their hope is the activities of those giant animals feeding, disturbing the soil, and spreading their manures across the plains would shift the biological balance away from the mosses and thin soils that supplanted the grasslands and back to the richer ecosystems that once dominated in that part of the world.

Some people speak of these budding and contemplated experiments almost as an obligation for humanity to restore the Earth's diversity that we so altered by our success as a species. Others ask if it is fair to bring creatures back to a world so different from that which they inhabited, especially when we seem unable to even properly serve as stewards of what remains. Pragmatists point out scientists might be able to master the broad strokes of shaping the living form of an extinct animal that once roamed our planet, but the millions of bacteria that lived within those creatures, helping them digest, breed, and survive, might not ever be reproducible, and so all would come to nothing but great expense. Some people find the whole idea scarier than Jurassic Park.

These are things that inevitably drift through one's mind when contemplating the history spread out before us at a place like the Kimmswick Bone Bed at the Mastodon State Historic Site in Missouri. The somewhat rural setting, on the edge of a major metropolitan area, with the familiar noises of distant automobiles and planes flying overhead contrast sharply with the silence of the long-gone majestic beasts who came to this place—drawn inexorably by forces of nature—and died where we may view their remains today. From whence did they come? Which way will we go? And how might our destinies be intertwined?

CHAPTER 9

The Three Springfield Women: Vanished

There are many unanswered questions in the case of the Three Springfield Women. The ache of not knowing must be what haunts family, friends, and investigators most. How do three women in a security-conscious household vanish without any sign of a struggle or any obvious motive for their disappearance?

Here is what is known:

On June 7, 1992, sometime after 2 a.m. Sherrill Levitt, Suzie Streeter, and Stacy McCall vanished without a trace. There have been no confirmed sightings or communications from any of them since. More than twenty years later, with over 5,000 tips leading investigators through twenty-seven states, the case remains unsolved and officially "cold."

Thirty officers with the local police department, plus the FBI, have worked the case as hard as they each knew how. The story has appeared on several national crime news shows and repeatedly on local radio and television programs. There are websites and blogs dedicated to the Three Springfield Women, turning over every lead and possible clue, examining suspects, and asking for tips. As with any case that has gone on as long as this one without resolution, there are plenty of people who disagree with how the case was handled and what, if anything, can or should be done now.

The clues left behind and agreed upon are tantalizing to a mystery buff, but a haunting brain burn to any professional whose job it is to figure these things out. To family and friends those "clues" are the last glimpses they have of loved ones: places and personal items that bring back memories and almost seem capable of bringing back the women themselves.

June 6, 1992, was graduation day for lots of kids, including Suzie Streeter and Stacy McCall. Both pretty and outgoing, they seemed to travel easily among a party crowd. Although Kickapoo High School had a well-organized and funded Lock Down program to keep the graduates out of trouble that night, Suzie, Stacy, and most of their friends apparently felt they knew how to have a better time. The girls and another friend made their way to at least a couple of parties, during which time plans for where they would spend the night changed more than once. Stacy had called her mother around 10:00 p.m. to say they planned to stay at their third friend's house with family. When that proved too crowded, Suzie and Stacy opted at about 2 a.m. to each drive over to the house where Suzie and her mom, Sherrill Levitt, had just recently moved. The next

Friends, relatives, and the police still welcome any tips to solve the disappearance of the three missing Springfield women.

day, the three girls planned to go with some of their friends to the White Water Amusement Park in Branson about an hour away.

The last conversation anyone is known to have had with Sherrill occurred somewhere between 9:30 and 10:00 p.m. when she spoke on the phone to a friend and talked about how she was refinishing a piece of furniture, as well as other plans for how she was going to fix up her new place. After those incidents, most people agree the three women were never heard from again.

The friend back where Suzie and Stacy had intended to spend the night got up around 9:00 the next morning and called to see what the plan was for getting to White Water that day. She intended to go over to Suzie's house to meet the girls there, but when nobody picked up the phone, she figured everyone was still sleeping. (Remember, this was in the days before cell phones, texting, and tweets.)

Later in the morning, the friend and her boyfriend drove over, expecting to find Suzie and Stacy and discuss their plans. When they arrived, Suzie's and Stacy's cars were in the driveway, and Sherrill's car was in the garage. The friends noticed the front porch light globe had been shattered, but there was still a working bulb in the socket. Not thinking much about it, the boyfriend apparently swept up the broken glass, to be helpful, while the girlfriend attempted to locate the girls or perhaps Suzie's mom.

Entering tentatively through the unlocked front door, the friends found nobody home except Sherrill's little dog. All three women's purses were neatly placed on the stairs, as if by habit. Tellingly, the packs of cigarettes Suzie and Sherrill chain smoked were there with their lighters, too. Both beds appeared to have been slept in; Suzie's king-size waterbed, which her mother gave her for graduation, would have been big enough for the two girls to share. One could see in the bathroom where Suzie and Stacy had removed their jewelry and makeup. Stacy's shorts were neatly folded, as if she intended to sleep in her T-shirt and underwear. Nothing seemed out of the ordinary, except the women's absence, so the friends moved about, innocently contaminating the crime scene, after which they eventually left. I suppose they thought the women might have uncharacteristically gone for a walk for some reason. Their minds weren't thinking of crimes.

Stacy's mom became worried when she did not hear from her usually dutiful daughter, but when she called the friend's home she learned the girls had not slept there. She did not have Sherrill and Suzie's new phone number, and it took her a while to track it down, along with the new address. When she received no answer, she finally went to the home in the late afternoon.

There seems to have been more comings and goings, with concerned or just curious friends dropping by, and certainly some of their visits might have overlapped. On that point investigators are not explicit in summaries given to the public, but everyone who visited the house seems to have been subsequently cleared by investigators. It was when Stacy's mom became increasingly worried by the apparent disappearances that she first called the police, approximately fifteen hours after they had last been seen.

An officer stopped by to perform a routine check of the premises, and left the residents a note to call the police station if they returned and wished to cancel the missing persons report. Someone on the phone from the police department had alarmed Stacy's mom further, by asking whether, if the women had not been located, she could perhaps bring along Stacy's dental records when she came to the station the next morning. There's just no "right time" to ask a mother that question.

Worry caused Stacy's mother to waste no time putting together her own missing persons flyer with pictures of all three women and a number to call. Once the case became the top local news story, where it remained for weeks, photos of the Three Springfield Women on a small poster appeared in store windows and on display boards all over town. They covered trees and telephone poles. Volunteers handed them out.

Tips poured in. Some were helpful. Many were not. Every lead had to be considered. Lots of tips were given more than once. Sometimes, when a tip is repeated, even after you think you've checked it out, it might be worth considering again. Cases like this always attract people who say they are psychic and calls that sound like parties of middle school kids calling for a prank. Good investigators nevertheless weigh everything carefully, and try not to close their minds when they close out a lead.

Suspects received a great deal of scrutiny. Some have been clearly ruled out, while others continue to draw attention. Crucial evidence is lacking.

Sherrill's son was at the time estranged from both his mom and his sister. Suzie and her brother had recently attempted to share a place together, but by his own admission his drinking and attitude caused her to move back in with her mom. Apparently both women agreed their lives would be better without him, if he was going to act badly. Investigators say he was completely cooperative, quickly revealing uncomfortable truths about his behavior back then, but giving no indication of a motive or anything other than appropriate concern that his family members be found. He passed the polygraph test he was given.

Suzie had given testimony against a former boyfriend a few months before, when he reportedly was investigated for cemetery vandalism and other crimes. Police seem confident Suzie had no advance knowledge of what her former boyfriend did. In interviews he drew extra scrutiny because he spoke disrespectfully of the women, but as time progressed he seemed to be ruled out as a suspect, too.

Two entirely different men now in prison continue to be persons of interest. Their comments, convictions, and confessions in other crimes keep them the focus of most people reconsidering the case today. The scenarios required for either of these two men to have been involved would seem to preclude the participation of both at the same time, so when they each give interviews appearing to lead investigators on, at least one or both of them must be lying. It is not uncommon for convicted serial killers to claim knowledge of other unsolved cases, offering information for a commuted sentence or immunity. Sometimes a plausible story will get a murderer out of prison and on a trip to another state, where the criminal suspect will enjoy the sunshine and fresh air while they tell investigators they can't quite remember if a body might be buried here or there. The case of the Three Springfield Women has been sufficiently well publicized to give someone wanting to make up a story plenty of details to work with if they wish.

The most often mentioned of these two criminals is Robert Craig Cox, now serving a life sentence in Texas for holding a gun on a twelve-year-old girl while committing a robbery. He will not be eligible for parole until 2025. Previously he was on Death Row in Florida after being convicted for the brutal beating death of Sharon Zellers, a nineteen-year-old Disney World clerk. That conviction was reversed by the Florida Supreme Court on the grounds evidence presented had created "only the suspicion" of guilt. Cox has also served time in California for abduction.

During the time the Three Springfield Women disappeared, Cox was living in Springfield with his parents while working as an underground utility contractor in the south and central parts of town. He claims to know the women are dead and says their bodies will never be found. In answer to a reporter's questions, he alledgedly told her that if he were wishing to abduct women in such a setting, he would go to the door and report a utility emergency. He has led people to believe he watched part of the investigative activity at the scene from across the road. According to some people, Cox has said he knows more about the case, information which he will exchange for immunity, but he has also said he would have more to say after his mother dies.

The other convicted criminal who has attracted attention is Larry D. Hall, currently serving a life sentence in Wisconsin after being convicted on federal kidnapping charges. Hall has reportedly confessed to at least thirty-nine abductions, indicating he killed some of his victims, but he has not been put on trial for any murders. (When an obvious suspect or confessed killer is already serving a life sentence, most prosecutors are unwilling to spend large sums from their limited budgets on complicated court cases, which can often carry the requirement of automatic appeals.)

Part of Hall's modus operandi was apparently to stalk victims at public places such as convenience stores, when traveling for his hobby as a Civil War reenactment soldier. Springfield has the nearby Wilson's Creek Battlefield, where Hall and his twin brother Gary attended a reenactment in 1991. A relative has made the statement the Hall brothers returned to the battleground in the summer of 1992. Reporters have written that Larry Hall has a low IQ of perhaps 80, as a result of oxygen deprivation at birth, but he possesses organizational abilities and worked as a janitor. Investigators searching for clues in his vehicle after one of his alleged crimes were surprised to find so few fingerprints or other normal evidence. The possibility he has worked with one or more accomplices is considered good by people who have interviewed him.

The reporter who seems to have done the most to keep the case of the Three Springfield Women in the mind of the public is Kathee Baird, whose award-winning *The Crime Scene* blog focuses primarily on major crimes and unsolved mysteries in Southwest Missouri. When she continued to hear tips from a variety of sources suggesting the women had been killed and buried on land now covered by a medical campus parking lot, she tried to interest the Springfield Police Department in conducting a search, which thus far they have declined to do. Baird went so far as to engage the services of Rick Norland, who used his detection equipment at Ground Zero in New York City to search for buried victims in the aftermath of 9/11. Norland's search with a ground-penetrating radar system came up with "three anomalies" that he will not categorically state are bodies, but which he says are "consistent with the images bodies could produce."

Statements made by investigators suggest they believe the time frame for bodies to be buried there is wrong, and such leads are from "crackpots and psychics." Apparently, even private offers to pay for digging and repair of the site have not gotten the job done. Many people express frustration, online and elsewhere, with the police department for not proceeding with a forensic dig, but not with the owners of the buildings where the parking lot is located.

Meanwhile, all of the other tips proffered to date seem to lead nowhere. Most tips came in after the case had received considerable publicity, which typically is when well-meaning people search their memories for anything they can think of that might be helpful, and other individuals might just want to be somehow involved in the highly publicized search.

A waitress said she remembered seeing all three women around 3 a.m. at a popular all-night restaurant Sherrill was said to frequent, but no other workers or patrons could confirm her account.

One person came forward about a month after the disappearances, saying a green or perhaps silver van had turned around in the person's driveway the morning of June 7, with a person matching Suzie's photograph at the wheel. Supposedly a man's voice was heard saying, "don't do anything stupid," and something like, "now just turn around and drive on out of here." Other tips mention a van having been seen in the area, ranging in color from green to silver to brown. Tips like these, when reported to the public, tend to generate more tips of a similar nature. That doesn't mean one or more of them might not be right.

Other potential leads seem to go nowhere. Robert Craig Cox worked as a mechanic for a while at the same car dealership where Stacy McCall's father worked, and he might easily have seen her stopping by to visit her dad there, but the time frame would have been before he took the job as a utility contractor, and she wasn't where anyone would have expected her to be sleeping the night of June 6.

Local news outlets went into overdrive on more than one occasion when preliminary forensic digs took place at wooded locations out of town, but nothing has come of those searches thus far.

It is impossible to read these accounts and not find yourself trying to imagine what might have happened. Questions abound.

In the vast majority of cases where people commit violent crimes, the perpetrators are people the victims know, if only slightly. In those rare instances when strangers commit violence against strangers, they are said by experts to experience greater gratification when the victim is perceived to be weak or vulnerable. Simultaneous abductions of adults are almost never committed by a single individual, and criminals who commit crimes together rarely remain loyal to each other for twenty years.

People close to the case say Sherrill was reasonably security conscious. A popular cosmetologist who has been described as having an active social life but "bad judgment" in men, she cannot have been naïve about the possibility of an old boyfriend or unwelcome acquaintance of her daughter barging into her home. People who visited the home after the disappearance said there was some kind of obscene phone call on the recorder, but it was reportedly accidently erased by Stacy's mom when she was trying to figure out where the women might be. No one has suggested that either Suzie's friend or Stacy's mom left messages on the phone when they called on June 7, and while this is perhaps an insignificant detail, it can leave one wondering.

Sherrill and Suzie had only been in their new place for a couple of months; it was in the middle of town, and not highly visible from the street. All those would be reasons for women living alone to keep doors locked and not let a stranger in late at night. Sherrill owned a small dog, which could come and go through a doggie door, but the animal has been described as agitated when people were around. It would seem hard, therefore, for someone to approach the house unannounced. However, even if the distant sounds of a barking dog could have woken a curious neighbor, few people would have thought that unusual in the city. A couple of blinds in one window were found parted, as if someone had been looking out. That, of course, could be explained by either Sherrill looking out when the girls finally got home, or something much more sinister.

Suzie and Stacy originally planned to drive to Branson after their graduation party and stay at a motel near White Water

Amusement Park. When they first changed their plans, they were going to stay at their friend's house, and only late that night did they decide to return to Sherrill and Suzie's home. If someone were stalking one or both of the girls, it is unlikely they would have been able to follow their progress and changing plans without leaving a witness sighting.

It seems more likely Sherrill would have been the first and only intended victim, but with complications arising when the girls arrived at the house unexpectedly so late at night. They clearly were not alarmed when they got home, because they took time to remove jewelry and makeup before getting ready for bed. Was Sherrill there to greet them, did they think she was sleeping, or was somebody else there whom they recognized, with a story about why they should not be alarmed if Sherrill was out of sight?

When did the globe for the front porch light get broken? Even if someone arrived home late, tired, and perhaps a little tipsy, wouldn't he or she take time to clean up the mess of broken glass, or at least scrape at the shards and push them to one side with a foot? Was the broken globe someone's failed attempt to put out the light quickly when the girls unexpectedly drove up, or a ruse used to create a diversion and draw the women away and outside one at a time? Someone could also have dropped the globe after removing it, in order to unscrew the light bulb and prevent the front light from working when someone came to the door.

Not a lot of kids move out of the house before they graduate from high school. The fact that Suzie tried to live with her brother might seem unusual, especially considering that reports consistently say the mother and daughter were very close. It's possible there had been a temporary rift between the two women that caused the separation. One also could question what might have occurred in either of their lives while they were living apart. A daughter that age might want to prove she is an adult, and a mom might do things when living alone she might not do with a daughter living at home. Did either of the women meet anyone during their separation who became the perpetrator(s) of this crime?

Moves are generally made for better opportunities or because of tight circumstances. People have said Sherrill was downsizing. If this was a good move, what was she leaving behind? Was Sherrill having a tough time, financially? If so, what might she have done to make extra money? Had she left people or a past she wanted to be rid of forever? Had she angered someone with something she knew or what she might say?

The case continues to baffle the best minds in criminal justice. Not long ago, investigators took a wealth of information they had collected to a large meeting of forensic professionals from around the country who try to give fresh perspective to old, cold cases. Still, no new developments are apparent.

We may never know what happened to Sherrill, Suzie, and Stacy. Or someone may come forward with the missing piece of information that makes the whole thing suddenly make sense. Imagine how wonderful it would be to make sense out of something so senseless.

CHAPTER 10

The Flight of the Atlantic: Fueled by Plenty of Hot Air

Sometime in the early hours of July 2, 1859, John LaMountain woke from pleasant dreams because he felt cold. Next he noticed his nose was bleeding. Although it was summer in the Midwest, the bucket of water he and his friends had brought along for their journey from St. Louis had begun to freeze. This was all perfectly understandable when you consider LaMountain and his companions suddenly found they were at an altitude well over two miles above sea level. From this point on, however, the details of the flight take on multiple trajectories, varying wildly from one account to the next.

LaMountain was an adventurous young aeronaut, eagerly hoping to learn from the more experienced aeronaut John Wise. Both men had independently been working on design improvements for balloon flight, and together they shared the dream of one day successfully crossing the Atlantic Ocean in a balloon. As

The crash landing of the *Atlantic* was spectacular, from all accounts.

was common in those days, both men frequently referred to themselves with the honorary title "Professor," although its application to either of them bore no relation to any university degrees. The flight they were on was considered a test (a trial balloon, if you will) for the flight they hoped they could continue sometime soon after successfully flying from St. Louis to New York. The flying ship in which they embarked was optimistically called the *Atlantic*. To demonstrate one of the many "practical" applications they envisioned for their experimental craft, they carried on board

123 pieces of mail sent without postmarks from St. Louis and addressed to various people in New York.

The two aeronauts' fellow traveling companions were O. A. Gager, an affluent balloon enthusiast from Vermont who had financed the construction of the *Atlantic*, and William Hyde, a reporter and future editor of the *St. Louis Republican*, who as far as anyone can tell had never previously been anywhere near a balloon. The wealthy Mr. Gager was given the largely ceremonial title of "Scientific Observer" with the reported purpose of studying whether there might be strong air currents moving from west to east in the upper atmosphere. Any such evidence would be somewhat anticlimactic; Wise and others had already discovered and reported such phenomena, although the details of such observations were not widely known to the general public. Gager's financial help was crucial to the aeronautical expedition, however, because Wise had also discovered he could not raise sufficient cash for his adventures simply by hovering over fair grounds in a tethered balloon and charging to drop dogs and cats down to their owners with parachutes he had designed specifically for the purpose.

John Wise actually made several more significant advances in balloon aeronautics by the time of this historic flight. Although he was not the inventor, he was the first person to successfully build and use a balloon that would convert the inflated envelope to a parachute shape if the flight needed to be aborted while high aloft. He invented or perfected several minor improvements in balloon and parachute designs, plus important changes like a better valve system for releasing excess gas and a rip panel to allow instantaneous deflation upon landing. Previously, fatalities had occurred when balloonists landed safely, but were then dragged for miles by their crafts. Yet another discovery credited to Wise was the degree to which the sun's rays could heat and expand the gases used in balloon flight (usually hydrogen or coal gas), so he pioneered the painting of balloon envelopes of the day black to maximize the advantage of this effect. Within a year of his first balloon flight in 1835, Wise flew from Lancaster, Pennsylvania, to Maryland in a balloon filled with hydrogen. When he was deflating the balloon amid a crowd of curious onlookers, a lantern ignited the volatile gas, severely burning Wise and several bystanders. He initially announced his retirement from aeronautics after the accident, but he had obviously caught the flying bug, because by 1837 he was flying again.

The *Atlantic* was launched from Washington Square in St. Louis at 7:20 on the evening of July 1, 1859. The envelope was most likely 130 feet tall and 60 feet in diameter (although some would have it larger). However large it was, the *Atlantic* created quite a spectacle for the crowd of thousands that had gathered. The fully inflated balloon had a lift capacity of between ten and twelve thousand pounds (although some claimed it was an unlikely twenty-five thousand pounds), which allowed generously for the weight of the passengers, bags of sand ballast, their luggage, provisions (including a bucket of lemonade plus several bottles of wine), books, and scientific instruments. Sixteen feet below the basket in which passengers normally traveled was suspended a five-hundred-pound wooden boat, in anticipation of a possible water landing, either on this flight or on the trans-Atlantic flight the men hoped would follow soon afterward. The boat was organized so the men could rest, reconnoiter, or recline there when not being more actively engaged in the basket above.

According to most reports, the launch was rather slow and uneventful at first, owing to the warm, still air of the lovely summer evening. Eventually the balloon drifted to the east and in due time was lost from sight of the city. As they gained altitude, their course shifted to the north and darkness made it impossible to determine their exact position. The two veteran balloonists and their benefactor, who by then had experienced a few balloon flights, felt calm and fell asleep, while William Hyde, the novice, stayed awake the longest, but then he, too, succumbed to slumber.

Accounts vary considerably, perhaps because the voyage did not turn out nearly as well as planned, and each man had his own agenda for what he hoped to accomplish in the future. Hyde may have been the most objective of the participants, albeit from the perspective of absolute ignorance regarding balloon travel before the journey began. Threads of the tale that have come down to us describing lapses or errors in judgment on the part of the experienced aeronauts may have been intended by Wise and LaMountain to disparage each other and gain favor with potential investors or future clients. Of all the stories, Wise's telling of the tale is the most vainglorious, filled with embellishments that cannot be substantiated, and rather dismissive of LaMountain's participation.

Hyde's story, given to a reporter with the *Buffalo Courier*, and republished in *The Union* July 13, 1859, tells of a rather uneventful night:

> Their motion was very rapid throughout the night, inclining rather towards the north, with calm beautiful weather. The aeronauts found it impossible to perceive their exact reckoning during the darkness, and went to sleep; but Mr. Hyde, to whom the situation was most novel, found himself unable to enjoy that luxury. Towards daylight, the altitude which they attained, between two and three miles, rendered the cold quite severe, but by no means painful, as they were well provided against such a contingency.

In an account published in *To-Day: The Popular Illustrated Magazine* in 1873, Wise wrote of a livelier and eventful first half of their flight. Wise claimed the balloon's envelope was initially misaligned within her ropes, and he called down to Mr. Gager, riding in the boat with Hyde and LaMountain, to come assist him make difficult readjustments, which left their hands sore and bleeding. This would be a not-so-subtle judgment against LaMountain, who was both the official builder of the balloon and its pilot. Wise, as "Director in Chief" outranked LaMountain, but it seems unlikely he would have called for the help of his wealthy patron and not his young fellow aeronaut to correct the problem.

Wise also wrote of an eerie luminescence within the balloon, lasting all night and not only enabling the men to witness remarkable scenes beneath them, but also giving them the opportunity to inter-act with people below. He gave an account of watching a fisherman who was supposedly pulling in his nets on the Wabash River after dark, but unable to discern from where people were calling out to him. Likewise, if we are to believe Wise's story, the men had a bit of fun with three drunks leaving a tavern and discussing their plans for returning home. There are other, highly fanciful descriptions of hearty hails the balloonists supposedly exchanged with a steamship captain and other boatmen as the balloon passed over two of the Great Lakes. All seems highly unlikely, given the altitudes described and our present-day awareness of how easy it is to discern a lighted object in the sky, especially if people up above are loudly calling down. Wise also made a few references in the piece to maintaining speeds of fifty or sixty miles per hour, which although probable, would make it virtually impossible to carry on the lengthy conversa-tions he described with so many individuals on land or water.

LaMountain, for his part, gave an account in which Wise, during his watch in the basket while the other men slept in the boat, carelessly let the lower opening of the envelope hang inside the basket where escaping gases supposedly rendered him uncon-scious. In his version of the journey, it was LaMountain who sent Hyde climbing to the basket, where he revived Professor Wise with fresh air, thus averting certain disaster.

Hyde, the reporter, mentioned none of those amazing, frightful, and accusatory details in his lengthy telling of the tale within a week of their landing, leading one to be much more inclined to believe his account that the first half of the journey went well and without incident. By 7 a.m. July 2 they were over Lake Erie, near Sandusky, and around noon "opposite Buffalo."

"In the last 100 miles on this lake, a current of air in which they floated gradually bore them to the water, until on several occasions their elevation did not extend 300 feet," Hyde told the Buffalo reporter. "Soon after the passing the [Niagara] Falls, the strength of this current rapidly increased, until they neared Sackett's Harbour. When over Lake Ontario, and about thirty miles from shore, it became a violent gale of wind, blowing almost directly downward." On this point, all participants seem to agree.

The story continued:

> Every effort was made to keep the balloon up, by throwing out ballast, stores, and instruments, but in spite of all their exertions, she made a tremendous dive, striking the water, staving the boat, and nearly bringing about a fatal termination of the voyage to Mr. LaMountain. The balloon then rushed headlong towards the shore, which was reached in a few minutes, from whence it plunged into a dense forest, at a speed which Mr. Hyde estimates at about two miles a minute.

Certainly, nothing can be proven just by taking sides in the disputes between Professors Wise and LaMountain, but suffice it to say in one man's version there was the necessity of two men climbing below the basket and chopping away at the boat in order to cast off pieces and raise the balloon above the water's surface. If one were going to do all that chopping, wouldn't it have been simpler to just cut the ropes? Here again, Hyde's less accusatory version seems more plausible, but no less harrowing.

"The grapnels were cast loose, but the strong iron hooks were wrenched off like pipe-stems. The boat, which was still below them, went crashing through the trees, leaving a path as if the locality had been visited by a tornado. Mr. Hyde says that trees a foot or more in diameter were snapped asunder as if made of clay, while the branches were flying in every direction. After proceeding about a mile at this rate, in momentary expectation of destruction, the balloon was dashed against a huge tree, by which it was collapsed, and scarcely anything left of it but countless ribbons. It seems marvelous that no lives were lost, but this was doubtless owing to the boat, which sustained the shock of the forest, leaving the daring adventurers to descend from their perch entirely unharmed, with the exception of a slight bruise which Mr. LaMountain received on one of his hips.

"Mr. Hyde speaks in the warmest terms of the kindness which they experienced at the hands of the people where they descended, and says that could he have been landed in safety the aerial ship would have completed her voyage to the Atlantic coast without difficulty. He regards the experiment as a success, as it is, and as fully demonstrating the feasibility of crossing the Atlantic ocean, by means of aerial navigation."

The newspaper story ends with the information Hyde left the little town of Henderson, New York, near where they crash landed on the farm of a Mr. Whitney. The newspaper indicates Hyde stopped briefly in Buffalo to give his account to a reporter with the *Buffalo Courier* before returning to St. Louis. The other men reportedly continued to Albany. Had I been William Hyde, a man with no previous experience in ballooning, and having just escaped such a violent flight with my life still preserved, I would have kissed the cow pasture beneath me, declared everyone within earshot my best friend for life, and then run as fast as my legs would carry me home, without stopping in Buffalo to file a report with my colleagues in the Fourth Estate.

From the passive-aggressive versions of the flight provided by Wise and LaMountain in the ensuing years and up until their deaths, one can only assume there was more yelling and screaming like a bunch of little girls aboard the *Atlantic* than anyone let on. O. A. Gager appears to have suddenly lost all his enthusiasm for ballooning. John LaMountain was reported to have "taken possession" of what was left of the *Atlantic* and used it to make a couple of short, reckless (although not wreck-less), and abortive hops toward the coast without ever getting there.

A month or so later Wise did make another well-documented attempted flight from the Midwest to the East Coast, this time in an airship christened *Jupiter*. On that flight, originating from Lafayette, Indiana, Wise carried an officially sanctioned and properly postmarked batch of mail, which he tossed overboard with a parachute, when he realized he might crash. Luckily, both the box containing letters and the balloon containing Professor Wise landed safely within 50 feet of each other, so Wise was able to deliver the mail to a mail train in nearby Crawfordsville, just thirty miles from his launch site. Because one of those postmarked letters was subsequently delivered to the person it was addressed to and survives to this day, the flight of the *Jupiter* is listed, officially, as the first use of air transport in delivery of postmarked mail in North America. One underwhelmed reporter covering the thirty-mile flight of the Jupiter rather snidely referred to it as an attempted "transcontinental" flight, although a flight from Indiana to the East Coast would scarcely cover a third of the distance across the continent.

The 123 letters Wise carried in his flight from St. Louis aboard the *Atlantic* were not formally postmarked in advance and were thrown overboard with all other nonessentials when the crew was attempting to gain altitude in the storm over Lake Ontario. Wise always claimed the crew of a passing ship found the floating mail and conveyed it to an official post office from where the letters were delivered, but none of those letters have been preserved, so his claims of an earlier transport of airmail are not widely accepted outside of St. Louis, where the flight of the *Atlantic* was commemorated with a plaque in Washington Square.

The flight of the *Atlantic*, however ill-fated, was sufficiently well documented to qualify as the longest balloon flight in world history to that time. The official record of 809 miles in nineteen hours and forty minutes stood for the next forty-one years. Not surprisingly,

Wise liked to stretch the claim to almost one thousand two hundred miles, and many unofficial reports give the distance generously as almost one thousand miles.

Both Wise and LaMountain were among the men who wished to be commissioned as chief aeronautical engineer for the Union Balloon Corps during the Civil War, but that distinction was granted by Abraham Lincoln to Thaddeus Lowe. None of the civilian balloonists were granted the military commissions they wished, but in a disorganized system, Lowe remained in charge. Perhaps the single point on which Wise and LaMountain ever found they were in complete agreement after their trip together aboard the *Atlantic* was their shared dislike for Thaddeus Lowe. Wise favored free-flight reconnaissance, which was rejected by Lowe in favor of tethered launches, and LaMountain was continually so vocal in his criticism of Lowe and others in the Corps that, in 1862, he was discharged by General McClellan himself from any further service to the army.

John LaMountain's later years are shrouded in mystery, with reports of a short, second marriage to a cousin, followed by divorce and a life alone in South Bend. One newspaper story mentioned his last flight as taking place in October 1869, on which occasion, supposedly, the crowd holding his balloon grew impatient and released his balloon prematurely. What followed was another extraordinary tale of rising to near fatal heights, at which point he was said to have torn a hole in his balloon's envelope with his teeth to allow gas to escape when the balloon's valve failed. After a crash landing that reporters said left the aeronaut "benumbed," he was said to have only survived a few months, dying in February 1870. Other biographies state he was not heard from after his brief Civil War exploits until his death was recorded in 1878.

John Wise's final flight was at the age of seventy-one in September 1879, just over twenty years after the flight of the *Atlantic*. On that occasion he lifted off from St. Louis in a balloon christened *Pathfinder* with passenger George Burr aboard. The two men were not heard from thereafter, but a month later Burr's body washed up on the Indiana shore of Lake Michigan. Neither John Wise's body nor any wreckage from *Pathfinder* was ever found. If half of his colorful claims for his long career as an aeronaut are true, perhaps he lived to a ripe old age among friendly natives on an undiscovered island in the mid-Atlantic. Wherever his body rests, John Wise will be, after Charles A. Lindbergh, perhaps the most mythic of all those who ever lifted off from the humble soils of Missouri, bound for the glorious skies above.

CHAPTER 11

Searching for Round Rocks and Stardust

Suddenly, and seemingly out of nowhere, Missouri was hit with three giant blasts. They probably occurred within moments of each other. The largest of these released almost four million times the energy contained in the atomic bomb dropped over Hiroshima during World War II. The biggest crater is about eleven miles in diameter, with fragments from the impact hurled over one hundred miles away. The land we call Missouri would never again be the same.

Only it was not called Missouri then. And it was not land, exactly, either; the entire area was covered by a vast, shallow sea. This was in a time older than Missouri, older than North America, older than dinosaurs and, yes, even older than a lot of dirt.

The time was more than three hundred million years ago, but the evidence still excites geologists and rock hounds today. The cause was most likely three meteorites striking what is now Missouri, but in the slow, careful way scientists proceed, many will only confirm the certainty of the first two of the three impact sites. The third and most exciting of the sites is still only deemed "probable" until a few more crucial bits of evidence can be found.

What excites scientists even more is that these Missouri craters, of which the "probable" Weaubleau-Osceola structure is the largest, are themselves part of what is known as the 38th parallel Anomaly. Unlike what the 38th parallel means to Korean War veterans, here stateside the 38th parallel Anomaly refers to a series of confirmed and probable meteorite craters stretching along the states of Illinois, Missouri, and Kansas. Scientists say, if the Weaubleau-Osceola structure can be confirmed as a definite meteorite impact site, "the argument for a serial strike [of meteorites] would be greatly strengthened if the ages of the other 38th parallel structures could be constrained to the same period as the Weaubleau structure."

Don't you just love the way science geeks talk? Translation: In the cosmic scheme of things, Earth, which is a pretty small target, was once hit with a bunch of meteorite birdshot, very likely pieces broken off the same asteroid. If you are one of those people who stay awake at night worrying about the possibility of an asteroid barreling down on us and destroying Earth as we know it, what can be learned from a serial strike might save our cheese. If you just like science or collecting rocks, this is still pretty cool.

To give you an idea of how rare a serial strike of meteorites on Earth would be, consider the other cataclysmic event of a similar nature that makes scientists perk up and put down their

Joshua Young

Round rocks formed long before there were dogs, or dinosaurs.

textbooks. They find it so memorable they can tell you exactly where they were when it happened. This other one took place, not on Earth, but on Jupiter, as a result of a collision with the comet Shoemaker-Levy 9 in July 1994. Jupiter survived, but received the planetary equivalent of a scratch on its face. The comet was not so lucky. But scientists watching (and you can view this on the Internet, too) saw the comet break apart in a series of spectacular colorful explosions that scattered it in a straight line and sent tiny remnants spilling across the Jupiter landscape. A collision of such magnitude was considered a once-in-every-6,000-years event, and the likelihood of something remotely similar happening on Earth is considered between 2,000 and 8,000 times less likely.

Thankfully, there aren't a lot of Shoemaker-Levy 9s out there to threaten us. Jupiter has been quaintly described as a "cosmic vacuum cleaner" for its ability to tidy up outer space. Because of its enormous size, Jupiter pulls in a lot of space "clutter" that would otherwise threaten our solar system's inner planets with missiles like Shoemaker-Levy and cannon balls like the one that apparently snuck through and struck Earth along our 38th parallel.

Of the meteorites known to have hit Earth, the one theorized to have hit and created the Weaubleau-Osceola structure would be in the top fifty worldwide and the fourth largest in the United States. If it was indeed just a piece of an asteroid that broke apart and is responsible for all the craters found along the 38th parallel, it was a big boy, indeed. And the scientific marvels do not stop there.

Strangely, however, only since the 1950s did scientists even realize there was anything unusual about the geology of the region around Osceola. Even when Dr. T. R. Beveridge did recognize back then there were rock formations that have been described as looking like what has been called "a pushed-together carpet," a meteorite strike was not suspected for decades thereafter. Geologists had spotted so-called "rock moats," which are concentric circles, in this case measuring miles across. Their best guesses seemed to be all related to some sort of ancient volcanic activity that they could not identify.

Then sometime before 2003, Dr. Kevin R. Evans, a geologist with Missouri State University, began suspecting there might be a crater within the strange formations near Truman Lake. He studied a series of topographical maps using Photoshop computer graphics without noticing anything particularly unusual, but when he grew tired and saved his work in a thumbnail size, the image he was seeking "just popped out."

The western edge of the crater borders the edge of Osceola, while the opposite side stretches along Weaubleau Creek, some eleven miles distant. Evans estimates the original crater may have been as much as 1,000 feet high, although three hundred million years of erosion and sediments filling in have taken a toll. The good news is that the site was rather quickly sealed in by sediments—over a million or a dozen million years or so—thus protecting what was there for better discovery and analysis today.

A meteorite large enough to create such a dent in Earth's surface would be approximately 400 meters in diameter, which some have likened to slightly more than twice the height of the Gateway Arch in St. Louis. Evans points out a meteorite that size, while massive, is less than half the size (one kilometer) that currently passes muster to be tracked by NASA as potentially dangerous to us little critters here on Earth. Let's just hope Jupiter keeps doing its job of sucking things up.

Now, please allow me to shift from my cheap dumbing down of what really is some incredible science to the other end of the telescope and time continuum regarding the big Missouri meteorite.

Back in the early 1940s, before geologists had even noticed there was anything particularly unusual about the rock formations in the area, two little boys were growing up on a farm near the little community of Vista, slightly southwest of Osceola and to the east of Weaubleau Creek. Like everyone else they knew, Bob and Bill Stiles noticed the rich, dark soil on their farm often revealed pretty cool round rocks. Please understand glaciers never made it down beyond what is now northern Missouri, so round rocks, especially rocks this round, were a curiosity. Without glacial grinding, most of the rocks in central and southern Missouri are big flat slabs or sharp little chips. Those round rocks really stood out as something unusual. Locals sometimes called them "dinosaur eggs" or "fish eggs," but nobody they knew really had any idea what they were. At the time, the Stiles brothers only knew they were fun to collect.

When Bob and Bill were not busy with the chores given to eight- and ten-year-old boys, or fishing, building forts, or doing any of the other things country kids do, the brothers enjoyed digging in the dirt and adding to their collection of the curious round rocks. One day they found something noticeably different. The object they discovered, which would obsess Bob especially to this day, was a larger-than-ordinary rock that seemed metallic and weighed, they guessed, about twenty pounds. Today Bob remains convinced it was a piece of a meteorite.

Since the boys were so young, the find only held their close attention for a little while. For a few days or weeks, the odd thing played into their fantasies and imaginings, but at that age they had no scientific frame of reference within which to place the heavier-than-normal rock. Other things eventually drew their attention. At a certain age girls became more interesting than rocks. There was more school. Eventually the boys' family moved away from the farm. They each married and had families of their own. No one knows what happened to that curious rock. But the memory of it kept nagging at Bob.

By nature Robert Stiles is more than a bit of a science guy. In college he pursued those interests and ended up working at the University of Tennessee for thirty-two years in biomechanics. At home he enjoyed an active family life and with his wife, Myra, Bob developed a passion for meticulously restoring a lovely old southern house. But always the memory of that strange rock back on the farm in Missouri nagged at him.

Whenever he would return for visits and family get-togethers, Bob would feel drawn by the mystery of what they had found. I doubt he could ever glance at someone's garden or yard collection of the locally familiar "Osceola round rocks" without thinking of the much stranger one that he let get away. His family maintained friendships with the people who now owned the property where he and Bill grew up, and they were glad to let him tromp around. He poked in the dirt and looked around at the land. And the memory of that mysterious rock nagged at him even more.

While most locals were only vaguely (if at all) aware of the scientific findings that began to reveal the extraordinary geological history of the place where they lived, Bob followed the gradual revelations with keen interest. Even before Kevin Evans made his important discovery, Bob was forming his own, somewhat similar, yet distinct, conclusions. By the time geologists and astronomers from all over the world were beginning to hear of the Weaubleau-Osceola structure, Bob was already obsessed.

Family reunions were held more often near Vista, so Bob could poke around and dig a little. When the relatives would gather for Memorial Day to decorate family graves in the vicinity, Bob would always make time to stop by the old farm to take a look around. As they grew older, his kids and their cousins were enlisted to help dig. When you married into the Stiles family, you got hitched to the meteorite mystery, too.

Lacking sufficient room in their large house for what he wanted as a private workroom/laboratory, years ago Bob hand dug a full basement out of cramped space he had under the house, which wouldn't let him stand up straight (the man is well over 6 feet tall). There he analyzed his own samples and sent others off for professional analysis. Now in his eighties, Bob, even with challenges from serious illness, has continued to dig.

Most scientists studying the "probable" impact site believe the meteorite would have been obliterated upon impact. Bob respectfully disagrees, and believes he knows approximately where at least a large portion of the historic space rock might be. He is so convinced pieces of the meteorite lie hidden underground on the farm where he grew up, he has paid for a series of exploratory investigations. First he hired someone to scan the land with ground-penetrating radar. He also had a company of consulting engineers take a 95-foot core sample, which he has closely analyzed himself. From that evidence he and his family have dug more by hand and with a rented auger.

Right now Bob Stiles is weighing his options for what may be next. If he can pluck from the ground something rare, the find would certainly capture worldwide attention. Watching his eyes sparkle as he tells the story of his lifelong quest, I doubt a find itself could be any sweeter than his search has been.

I compare it to when people over on nearby Truman Lake talk about fishing. Some of them will tell you, "Oh, I like to fish, when the fish are biting." True fishermen will tell you those guys do not really like to fish. Bob Stiles is casting a line into the universe every time he digs down a little ways on the old family farm. Now there is a guy who really likes to fish.

For those of us who only like to fish when the fish are biting, the pastime of hunting "Osceola round rocks," also variously known as "Missouri rock balls" or "Weaubleau eggs," is about as close to finding meteorites as we are ever going to get. Look around the yards and gardens of people who have lived in the wider region surrounding the Weaubleau-Osceola structure for any time at all, and you will likely see the evidence of how fun it is to angle for round rocks. Round rocks form borders of sidewalks and garden beds. Round rocks sit stacked in ornamental piles. For a hundred years and more, locals have used round rocks to build and ornament walls, well houses, porch posts, stair steps, and benches. Visitors to the area carry the curiosities far away to serve as doorstops and paperweights back home.

Round rocks commonly range from the size of a golf ball to something resembling a softball or even a large grapefruit.

Occasionally one will be unearthed that is the size of a bowling ball. The shape, while never quite perfect, is generally well-rounded or ovoid. One small surface will usually be flat.

The fancy names for round rocks are alternately "post-impact chert concretions" and (my personal favorite) "spherical nodules of chert that nucleated around siltstone clasts." What that means, for starters, is when the meteorite hit the shallow ocean, it immediately vaporized the water in the area of the crater, simultaneously throwing up many cubic miles of superheated mudstone and pea-gravel-size blue-green shale (quintessential smithereens). The shale fell back to Earth, where it lay bathed in mineral-rich waters that gradually formed deposits around the gravel bits. "Somewhat like the way pearls are formed around a bit of grit," is the way one educated layman described the process.

Round rocks have been mistaken by some people for geodes, but the process of formation is actually somewhat the opposite. Whereas geodes dissolve from the inside to form a hollow core, round rocks build outward around a central shale seed and remain solid. Some people like to break open round rocks in the hope of finding fossils, but that possibility is rare, and the results rather boring for most of us when compared to the crystal formations exhibited within geodes. With so many rock hounds avidly searching for round rocks, there are those who theorize someday they may be exceedingly hard to find. I have found online postings where people even offer to pay for the privilege of hunting round rocks on someone else's property. For my part I have two or three given to me by good friends from Osceola, and I prefer to leave my node stones unturned.

A few years ago the highway department widened Highway 13, running north and south just east of the Weaubleau-Osceola structure. This was a bonanza for rock hounds, and although most of the best foraging has been done, travelers can still see odd fellows and game gals scrambling along the faces of eroded cutaways, picking out round rocks and searching for more rock riches in the ditches.

However much we scratch at the surface of what happened more than three hundred million years ago here on this piece of Earth we now call Missouri, much of it still remains hidden from view and ripe for study. Whether it is an old lady who just wants a few more round rocks to complete her flower garden border, Bob Stiles searching for the meteorite itself in a place he called home, or Dr. Evans seeking to learn and teach the overall forces of the universe that shaped our world, each person drawn to this place finds fascination in nature. Others drive by on the highway, with music blasting, thinking only of their destination and where they can find the cheapest gas. I try to remember there are mysteries all around us and hope to remain receptive to their truths.

On his professional page for the Department of Geosciences at Missouri State University, Dr. Evans posted what he calls:

Four Noble Truths of Geology

(. . . with apologies to His Holiness the Dalai Lama)

The Earth is dynamic.

The Earth is very old.

Life has evolved on Earth.

Humans exist in a perilous geological environment.

He goes on to describe how they came about:

A few years ago, half a dozen books got soaked from watering plants on my bookshelf. Spreading the books out to dry, I noticed my copy of the *The Four Noble Truths* was damp. I'm not a Buddhist (not a practicing one anyway), but it struck me that if truths are transcendent, are there truths we recognize in geology?

"Scientists commonly express the most highly probable relationships as laws or principles, but there must be truths as well. I have seen these ideas mentioned in other terms, but these seem succinct and relevant.

I wonder how many other professors of geoscience can work a little Buddhism into their thought and teaching? I think his students must be lucky indeed.

CHAPTER 12

Jesse James Lives On in Infamy

The morning of April 3, 1882, was unseasonably hot in St. Joseph, Missouri. Jesse James had moved to a house near where he had been born, and despite his widespread reputation as an outlaw, many people in town were proud to call him their friend. The notorious militias and gangs Jesse once rode with and occasionally led were disbanded or defeated; most of their members were dead. Paranoid from constant pursuit, Jesse only trusted the brothers Charley and Robert Ford, who were living with Jesse and his family at the time. Charley had ridden with Jesse on a few robberies; Bob had recently joined as a young recruit.

Jesse had no idea Bob received communications from then-governor Thomas T. Crittenden, promising the Ford brothers $5,000 each for the capture of Jesse and Frank James. The Missouri legislature had recently tilted back toward closer favor with Southern sympathizers and reduced the amount the governor could offer in rewards. Working around the legislature, Crittenden went to the railroad and express corporations the James brothers robbed to raise a reward sufficiently tempting to induce someone on the inside to risk confrontation with the notorious outlaws. Only Jesse was still living in Missouri. Frank thought it safer to move to Virginia.

Normally, the callow Bob Ford would have been no match for the seasoned killer Jesse James. Instead, he waited until Jesse's guard was momentarily down. The three men saddled their horses in order to be ready to ride out on a robbery they planned. Jesse took off his coat because of the heat and removed the guns it concealed, in order to avoid attracting attention from the neighbors. Back inside, Jesse noticed a framed piece of embroidery his mother made for him was dusty. Because she was planning to visit later in the day, the dutiful son stood on a chair to dust the frame and straighten it. Bob Ford took the opportunity to shoot Jesse through the back of his head. You can still see where the bullet entered the wall if you visit the Jesse James Home Museum in St. Joseph.

There is no mystery left about the death of Jesse James. The fact he was a mythic figure of the American West is well-known. What still baffles and disturbs many people is how a cold-blooded killer, a racist, who openly bragged of his robberies and murderous exploits, could be celebrated so widely as a Robin Hood hero, even to this day. Can there be any lessons in the life of Jesse James we have not yet learned?

Jesse Woodson James was born September 5, 1847, near Kearney, Missouri. He was the middle child of three. Frank was

At seventeen, young Jesse James clearly was eager to join the Confederate cause.

his older brother and he had a younger sister, Susan Lavenia James. The family was prosperous. Robert S. James was a Baptist minister and farmer from Kentucky, who moved to Missouri after marriage to Zerelda Elizabeth Cole James. One of Robert James's notable accomplishments in Missouri was to help with the founding of William Jewell College in Liberty.

Clay County, where the James family lived, was in the heart of Little Dixie. The region was dominated by slave-holding families from the South. In this Robert James was fairly typical, owning one hundred acres and six slaves. During the California Gold Rush, Robert James traveled to California with the stated intention of ministering to gold miners, but he died there soon after he arrived when Jesse was only three years old. Jesse's mother married twice more during his childhood, settling back on the James farm with Dr. Reuben Samuel when Jesse was about eight years old. With her third husband Zerelda had four more children, and the farm remained a slave-holding tobacco farm.

Whereas slaves in the entire state of Missouri constituted only about 10 percent of the population, in Clay County slaves were a hefty 25 percent minority. As the Civil War approached, considerable conflict arose as to whether the western territory of Kansas would be free or slave holding. Many landowners from Little Dixie moved west of Missouri with their slaves—thinking to control the issue—but antislavery factions were also becoming well established and conflicts flared.

The Civil War opened with battles between conventional armies in Missouri, but as those armies became entrenched and the focus of the war shifted more to the East, much of the fighting in Missouri and border regions was carried out by guerrilla fighters and local militias. Secessionist "bushwhackers" battled with

Union-affiliated "jayhawkers," with both groups traveling back and forth across the Missouri/Kansas border. Terrible atrocities were committed on both sides.

Frank James had joined a local company and traveled to fight in the (Springfield) Battle of Wilson's Creek, but he was too ill to continue and returned home. By 1863 he was being sought by Union forces as a member of a Confederate guerrilla band. When a Union militia came to the James/Samuel farm looking for Frank, Dr. Samuel was tortured and teenage Jesse was whipped.

Attacks only escalated when Frank joined with Quantrill's raiders, participating in the massacre of two hundred men and boys in the abolitionist stronghold of Lawrence, Kansas. In 1864 Frank returned to Clay County, where he and young Jesse joined first one and then another guerilla squad. Together they were said to have been involved in the Centralia Massacre, in which twenty-two unarmed Union troops were killed or wounded, with many scalped and dismembered. A regiment of Union troops that came to attempt a rescue was ambushed by the guerillas, and when one hundred men attempted surrender, all were killed. Jesse and Frank were identified as being among those who shot the soldiers and their commander. Sometime during those hostilities, Jesse received the first of two serious chest wounds he would suffer during the Civil War.

As a result of Frank and Jesse's guerilla activities, Union officials ordered the James/Samuel family to move south of Union lines, but they disobeyed the order and fled to Nebraska. When their commander was ambushed and killed, Frank and Jesse joined different armed groups in Kentucky and Texas, respectively. Jesse returned to Missouri the following spring, where he received his second life-threatening chest wound while attempting to surrender when confronted by Union troops.

With the Civil War soon officially ended, Jesse went to live at an uncle's boarding house in Kansas City, where he was tended by his cousin "Zee." After a nine-year courtship, the couple eventually married. Together they had two children who survived to adulthood.

Missouri remained bitterly divided after the Civil War. Political parties divided into antislavery Republicans, segregationist Democrats, and former Confederate secessionists, some of whom found alliances with the conservative Democrats. As was true in the Deep South during Reconstruction, efforts were made to disenfranchise former secessionists, at least temporarily, but within a few years they found their way back into powerful political positions again.

The James brothers, with their family's fortunes devastated and their hearts bitterly hardened against those they considered oppressors, elected to continue open, violent crimes against those individuals and organizations they blamed. No longer able to be slave holders, the James brothers remained adamantly pro-slavery; so much so, Jesse was heard to promise he would shoot any black man he encountered who was acting in any way other than a proper slave should.

In February 1866 they were said to have committed the first armed daylight robbery of a bank in the United States during peacetime (although "peacetime" in those early days after the Civil War was a relative term). The bank was owned by a Republican who had been a militia officer and who had just committed the audacious offense of holding the first Republican Party rally ever held in Clay County. As they made their escape, an innocent student from the college their father helped found was shot dead.

Jesse's former commander in Texas, Archie Clement, also had trouble accepting the new order, and went so far as to take a group of men to occupy Lexington, Missouri, on Election Day in 1866. Governor Thomas C. Fletcher ordered the state militia to rein in the guerilla groups, and Clement was soon killed. Later Jesse would write of the action as an affront to justice.

Evidence suggests Frank and Jesse rode with Clement's gang, as it came to be called, and even though the band of outlaws suffered many losses through shootings, executions, and arrests, they remained active. In later attempts to place their actions in a favorable light, they claimed to have robbed large banks that represented corporate interests back East, but researchers examining the evidence find otherwise. While robbing the small-town bank of Richmond in 1867, the gang shot and killed the mayor and two others.

Two years later Jesse's exploits finally gave him publicity, when he (and likely Frank, too) pulled off a small robbery of a bank in Gallatin, Missouri, where Jesse coldly shot a cashier after mistaking the man for the militia officer who had killed one of his Civil War guerilla commanders, "Bloody Bill" Anderson. Although the negative publicity elicited widespread condemnation of Jesse James, and branded him for the first time in the press as an outlaw, it also probably brought him to the attention of John Newman Edwards, the founder and editor of the *Kansas City Times*.

Edwards fought for the Confederacy and sought openly to return secessionists to power in Missouri after the war. In 1870 he published the first of many letters from Jesse James, giving the outlaw a forum from which he could claim to be fighting corrupt officials of the Union cause. Gradually Edwards used his editorials to amplify James's rants, and he portrayed him as a last vestige of Confederate virtue.

Edwards found his first good opportunity to do this after Jesse and Frank robbed the ticket office of the Kansas City Industrial Exposition in 1872. Although they netted a little less than a thousand dollars in the daring holdup, they would have gotten about $12,000 if they had arrived a few minutes earlier. The three masked men (Frank, Jesse, and an accomplice) held off a crowd of ten thousand spectators at closing time, but one of them fired a shot as they made their getaway and wounded a girl in the leg.

According to historian T. J. Stiles in his book *Jesse James: Last Rebel of the Civil War*, Edwards used the occasion of the Exposition robbery to portray Jesse James as a modern-day Robin Hood, supposedly robbing from the rich, Northern industrialists who he said bankrolled the occupation of the South during

Reconstruction. Although there is no evidence Jesse, Frank, or members of their gangs ever shared any of their stolen cash with anyone outside their inner circle, Edwards left readers with the impression they did. There were plenty of former Confederates and Confederate sympathizers in and around Kansas City at the time, but this nevertheless demonstrated a marked shift toward support for the unrepentant outlaws.

Soon after the Exposition holdup, the James brothers joined Cole Younger and his three brothers with other former Confederates to establish what became known as the James-Younger Gang. There seems to have been shared leadership in decisions made by the gang, but Jesse James was the recognizable face and name, so he gained in fame as the group grew bolder.

After a series of robberies stretching from West Virginia to Texas and as far north as Iowa, in 1873 the gang derailed the Rock Island train in Adair, Iowa, and pulled off their first train robbery. Their notoriety often gets them mention as the first train robbers in US history, but that dubious distinction goes to the Reno brothers in 1866, and there were several that followed in between. The James-Younger Gang holdups were notable for the fact they wore Ku Klux Klan masks that reinforced their image as idealistic Confederates, fighting Reconstruction and wealthy Northerners, while upholding Southern virtues and white supremacy.

In their first robbery the gang killed the engineer and several passengers, while stealing the contents of the safe and passengers' possessions, too. In their next couple of train robberies, they continued to steal from passengers, but they soon seemed to realize their reputations would suffer. Thereafter stories spread, no doubt encouraged by Edwards and the *Kansas City Star*, that the James-Younger Gang would "spare any man with calloused hands and all women," although one account survives of them relieving a woman of $400 in gold coins.

The Pinkerton Detective Agency was hired by the Adams Express Company in 1874 to put an end to the rampage of the James-Younger Gang. Chicago-based Pinkerton was more experienced in preventing urban crime and union busting, so they made several mistakes in attempting to track down members of the gang in territory sympathetic to the Confederate cause. Two agents and a local deputy sheriff were killed, although John Younger was killed, too, in the process. At that point Allan Pinkerton himself took charge and joined with local Unionists to stage an assault on the family homestead. The attackers firebombed the house, killing Jesse's half-brother Archie, and blowing off one of his mother's arms. Although Pinkerton denied that was his intention, biographers have found otherwise, and the horrific act fueled even more hatred of corporate interests and authority. Edwards had a field day with negative publicity, and Jesse's fame and support continued to grow.

Such was the support for the James-Younger Gang after the Pinkerton raid, that the Missouri legislature, which was by now filling with returning ex-Confederates, nearly granted amnesty to the gang. What the changing legislature did do was to lower the amounts of rewards the state of Missouri could pay for the apprehension of criminals, thus granting a measure of protection to the entire gang.

In 1876 the James-Younger Gang staged an aborted robbery on the First National Bank of Northfield, Minnesota, in which several people, including two of the robbers, were killed. An ensuing manhunt resulted in the capture of all of the remaining gang members except Jesse and Frank.

The James brothers lived quietly for a time under aliases in Tennessee. Frank seems to have decided to leave his life of crime, but Jesse returned to Missouri, recruited a new gang, and went on a multistate crime spree from Missouri to Alabama. The gang members were less experienced than Jesse's previous cohorts, so soon they were apprehended or got into disputes with each other. Jesse appears to have become paranoid at that point, threatening one remaining gang member and possibly killing another. His last crime spree seems to have lasted until 1881, when both Frank and Jesse returned to Missouri together. Frank did not stay long and soon moved to Virginia.

When Bob Ford shot Jesse James, a crowd gathered immediately as word spread. Ford telegraphed the governor to claim his reward, and both brothers turned themselves in, but they were immediately charged with murder. Within a day they were indicted, allowed to plead guilty, sentenced to be hanged, and two hours later pardoned by the governor. The governor's quick pardon suggested to many people he never expected Jesse to be taken alive, but the rush to sentencing also suggests local authorities

LIBRARY OF CONGRESS, LC-USZ62-3854

Although still handsome at 35, Jesse James was an ugly racist and a cold-blooded killer.

wanted to hang the men who had done the governor's bidding and killed their local heroes.

The Ford brothers received only a small portion of the reward, with the majority going to two law enforcement officers who had been involved in the plan. The Fords briefly went on the road in states more favorable to the Union cause, acting out the shooting of Jesse James. Within two years Charley committed suicide. Bob Ford ran a tent saloon in Colorado until 1892, when a man entered, said only "Hello, Bob," and shot him point blank with a shot gun. Edward O'Kelley was sentenced to life for the crime, but a seven thousand-signature petition caused the governor to pardon him ten years later. Such was the lasting legacy of Jesse James.

Rumors that Jesse had somehow survived continued to persist until his body was exhumed in 1995 and DNA analysis proved it was indeed his. Since his death, Jesse James's life and legend have been re-created by countless books, more than thirty films, and at least six television dramas. Today there are half a dozen festivals dedicated to his memory or exploits and as many museums doing the same. He has been portrayed extensively in comics, songs, and stage presentations.

Why would a cold-blooded, racist killer receive such attention? For many Jesse James represented the last resistance of the Confederacy. Through his letters to the *Kansas City Times* he was able to communicate directly to that audience and there found a supportive editor who amplified his message and mythologized his exploits. The white leadership of the antebellum South created in their heroic portrayal of Jesse James a simple, handsome young man who was disenfranchised, but who responded by wreaking havoc upon his epic enemies. In the tradition of Robin Hood, Jesse

James represented an American strain of what has been termed "social banditry," even in the face of overwhelming evidence that his aims were selfish and cruel.

There was no Truth and Reconciliation Commission after the Civil War. Despite the best intentions of Abraham Lincoln, the Reconstruction imposed after the war attempted to grind a defeated South further into submission. Without any mechanism by which all sides could confess their abominations of war and seek forgiveness, the spirit of rancor and hatred festered and grew. The atrocious acts Jesse James committed gave voice to the anger and desire for revenge that lay in so many Confederate hearts after the battles and raids were over. Missouri, with her deeply divided population, almost perfectly reflected divisions within the country itself.

Today sometimes we feel so far from the atrocities of our own Civil War, we look with horror at other countries or regions where racial, religious, or resource differences divide and embitter people, causing some to commit unspeakable acts. When we allow ourselves to celebrate, even briefly, such a tragically flawed and emotionally scarred, albeit fascinating individual, do we not tragically diminish ourselves?

CHAPTER 13

Earth Light, Earth Bright, Hope I See a Light Tonight

arth Lights. Spook Lights. Ghost Lights. Devil's Lanterns. Whatever names they go by, these inexplicable spectacles have been appearing to all manner of audiences in extreme southwest Missouri over the past 130 years at least. Some people say sightings of the strange phenomenon near the little cluster of houses once known as Hornet, Missouri, date back as far as the 1830s. Native Americans will tell you their ancestors spoke of the mysterious lights long before white settlers ever arrived.

Today Hornet is, practically speaking, a ghost town. You have a better chance of seeing the Hornet Spook Light, itself, than seeing anything you would recognize as a town where Hornet used to be. Plenty of other communities are glad to be associated with a phenomenon that has been bringing curious visitors to the region for more than a century, so you will hear the names "Spooklight" (alternately written as two words about half the time) or "Ghost

Light" (either as one word, or two) prefaced by place names such as Joplin, Seneca, Quapaw, Neosho, and Ozark. Like the generic "Ozark Spooklight" (named for the region, not the city), the name "Tri-State Spook Light" for years was frequently used and popularized even further as the title of a little tourist booklet people used to sell. All three states of Missouri, Oklahoma, and Kansas that come together in the Tri-State area are proud to be associated with the Spook Light, although I can find no reference to the lights ever appearing just to the north in Kansas.

Like many people who are not originally from around here, I was doubtful. The first person who ever confirmed the truth of earth lights for me was a devout Methodist in his eighties who had a solid reputation for always telling the truth. He'd been going down to watch the Hornet Spook Light since he was teenager. Another man I know said his parents used to give the kids the choice of, "Do you want to go to the drive-in movie, or go see the Joplin Spook Light?" They had seen the Spook Light so many times by then, as often as not, they would vote for the drive-in movie. If the date was closer to Halloween, though, the Spook Light would likely win out.

Closer to Halloween you will hear more of the spooky explanations for the mysterious lights that float and hover close to the ground or sometimes above the treetops. One tale says the lights, which can divide and seem to recombine, are the spirits of a young Quapaw couple who jumped from a nearby cliff called the Devil's Promenade overlooking the Spring River. Theirs was a

Romeo-and-Juliet-style romance that had been forbidden by their families. Different stories involve headless miners or Civil War soldiers who are searching with a lantern for their missing noggins. A few variations tell of parents searching for missing children. I guess it depends on who you want to spook that particular night.

The first recorded account of the earth lights in the area dates back to 1881 in a publication titled *Ozark Spooklight* by Foster Young (no relation to me). Either because of the interest generated by that publication, or for other reasons undetermined, in 1886 there appears to have been an inordinate number of sightings in the fields around Hornet. There have been accounts by locals who claimed sometimes the lights were bright enough to work by. A farmer claimed he didn't need his lantern to milk one night. Another man told his grandson the light he witnessed in 1910 one dark night was so bright, "I could count the buttons on your granny's dress."

The lights frightened some early settlers enough that they moved away. Braver and more practical folks seem to have just accepted the mysterious earth lights like the beautiful mysteries of fireflies and shooting stars. Now we know (or can Google, if we've forgotten) the "what, why, and how" of fireflies and shooting stars, but nobody can tell you for certain what causes the earth lights along the Missouri/Oklahoma border. Plenty of people have tried.

"Anomalous light phenomena" will open the topic pretty well, if you want to sound scientific. "Anomalous" is just a two-dollar, science geek name for *abnormal* or *bizarre*. "Light" you probably more or less understand, as long as we don't have to get into wave lengths, Einstein's Theory of Relativity, and String Theory. "Phenomena" is just the plural of things you notice but don't understand well enough to call something else. So we start out with knowing we have got some kind of weird lights out there that people have noticed and that we don't understand.

Educated guesses about the source of these anomalous light phenomena (after we toss out the aforementioned ghosts, spooks, and devils) include swamp gas (basically methane), fox fire (phosphorus), ball lightning (not likely, because this often happens on cloudless nights), seismic luminosity (electrical sparking from minerals rubbing together underground), highway billboards (think MacDonald's), or reflections from automobile headlights.

The latter theory was popular with a writer for *Popular Mechanics* who visited in 1965 and claimed the lights were coming from Route 66, some ten miles away. He said the shimmering or hovering effects were due to varied temperatures in layers of air above the ground. Locals scoffed at that idea after the magazine hit the newsstands. They said, "We want to get that science guy back to explain to us where the lights had been coming from during all those decades before automobiles." *Popular Science* was not popular with Spook Light fans for quite a while after that.

A different science guy, Professor Henry H. Hicks, with the Department of Mechanical Engineering at the University of Arkansas, also witnessed the earth lights and, when dismissing the un-*Popular Mechanics* theory, noted somewhat dryly, "I rather doubt that atmospheric refractions could cause the effect [because] refractions are subdued at night." That statement would have been enough to get Professor Hicks high fives all around on Spooklight Road some dark night, if he hadn't gone on to suggest the light, in his opinion, "is some kind of fixed light, perhaps a billboard light, [but] some of the mechanisms are not clear." Oops. That's not the way to win friends and influence people who love their Spook Light.

So, let's go back to the top of the list and consider the possibility of swamp gas or fox fire. Swamp gas can generate some pretty weird lights, but conditions around Hornet don't quite seem to fit. Add to that the ability of these lights to move, hover, and zip far away sometimes, and it makes the possibility of swamp gas seem to me (admittedly a nonscience guy) slim to none. Likewise, fox fire is caused by an abundance of phosphorus, usually on a wet, rotting log. One cause is when foxes or dogs keep peeing on the same rotting log to mark their territory. If conditions are right, the abundance of phosphorus in urine collects and makes an eerie glow at night. We would occasionally come across fox fire in the woods when I lived in New Hampshire. It is weird stuff, certainly, but fox fire does not move from the spot, as far as I know, except for the time we smeared some on the back of Joey's hoodie, and that night he made it fly like the wind.

So what are we left with? Seismic luminosity or a big "I don't know." Because I don't like to say I don't know, my vote is for seismic luminosity. That happens when the movement of rocks, minerals, crystals, and ores underground cause unusual electrical sparks, currents, or discharges that can be discerned by the light emitted. An extreme version of this can be witnessed sometimes during earthquakes (see chapter 6 on the Great Quakes of New Madrid). During a big earthquake, discharges of seismic luminosity can look a lot like lightning. Sometimes witnesses have described a "ball lightning" effect, and stranger illuminations, large and small, too.

The ground in the vicinity where people see the earth lights near Hornet contains lead and zinc ores, like much of the wider region, which was originally settled by miners. It is also a region of minor seismic activity, much of it too slight to detect without scientific instruments. The area also borders a region, particularly to the west, which is rich with coal and oil deposits. Lead and zinc ores are frequently mentioned among those that can generate seismoluminous effects. Perhaps these alone or in the presence of the right mix of oil shale or coal ore, might do what it takes when it shakes.

I have read that the same concept of seismic luminosity that can be observed in a major earthquake is what generates the spark in many cigarette lighters and those butane wands some people use to light a charcoal grill. Have you ever seen a spark fly off from a cigarette lighter? I'm not a smoker, but I've seen it happen. Sometimes the spark will seem to live a moment longer than you expect. I wonder if the earth lights might be something akin to a giant version of those sparks. But what do I know? I'm just a guy.

If you want to really obsess over these phenomena you may wish to check out the International Earthlights Alliance formed in

2003 by Dr. Marsha Adams and Professor Erling P. Strand, with lots of support and input from others, ranging from brainy scientists to delightful whackos (and sometimes you get two mints in one). On their website, www.earthlights.org, you will find things like a list of well over a hundred names associated with earth lights ("foo fighters" and "ignis fatuus" are a couple of my personal favorites). They present all kinds of theories, ranging from those of physicist Dr. David Fryberger of Stanford Linear Accelerator fame, who postulates a subatomic particle called the "vorton" might be involved, down to unnamed people who suggest "glowing bunnies" could have been running through phosphorescent minerals to cause the effect. (Remember my friend Joey, running through the woods with a gob of fox fire on his sweatshirt?)

The IEA (that as an acronym sounds a little like what Joey was screaming that night) goes into real scientific depth, which I like, even when some of the science is over my head. They explain things very well. At the same time they are not shy about putting some of the fringe theories on the table (think glowing bunnies). And just maybe a goofy idea holds a grain of truth, or sparks a good idea. On their website you'll also see information specific to other earth light sites, such as the ones in Marfa, Texas, and Hessdalen, Norway.

In the 1940s the Spook Light was investigated by both a group of students from the University of Michigan over a two-week period, and the Army Corps of Engineers from nearby Camp Crowder, following World War II. I found no details of the methodology employed by these investigators, other than the facts that the students had tried shooting the lights with a high-powered rifle (that only caused the light to blink out and reappear), and the Army engineers tried to demonstrate the lights were indeed caused by automobile headlights. Unfortunately, others reviewing the Army's inconclusive findings determined they had probably been looking down the wrong road.

Until 1962 there was a little general store in Hornet where people could stop and get directions and snacks from the proprietors, Olivia and Bud Buzzard. (I guess the Army engineers did not stop by there.) The Hornet store was one of the places where, for twenty-five cents, you could buy a copy of the little *Tri-State Spook Light* booklet authored simply by "Bob."

In the mid-twentieth century, a shack called the Spook Light Free Museum, or sometimes the Spooksville Museum, was built by Arthur Posie Meadows, a self-described photographer and the "Mayor of Spooksville." The "museum" was located at the intersection of County Road E 50 and State Line Road, which separates Missouri and Oklahoma. Those in the know say the museum was later run by Leslie W. Robertson, who later sold it to his brother-in-law Garland "Spooky" Middleton, a cheerful, grizzled old guy who donned the mantle of Mayor of Spooksville and ran the place as late as the 1970s. There was a viewing platform, where for a dime you could look for the Spook Light through a telescope. In its latter days the museum was expanded to include a pool table and a bar. Not many joints in such an isolated location would find it profitable to stay open after dark, but thanks to the Spook Light (and perhaps the aforementioned bar) the museum had hours from 6 p.m. to 1 a.m. and reportedly boasted 271 visitors on one night alone. The place fell into disrepair after Spooky died, and fire reportedly wiped out all but the foundation and a few fond memories. Now the site is said to be a private residence.

Spooky once told Dale Kaczmarek, ghost researcher and president of the Ghost Research Society, he

> remembered that [once] the Spook Light appeared on the road just after sunset and began to roll like a basketball giving off sparks as it tumbled down the gravel road. It then entered into a grassy field where several cows were quietly grazing away. It appeared to move silently among the cattle without disturbing them one bit! In fact, the animals paid no attention to [their] illuminated visitor at all!

Suzanne Wilson, a writer with some apparent family connections nearby, wrote an excellent article on the Spook Light for the *Missouri Conservationist* in 1997, revised online in 2010. In it she sums up the kind of sightings most witnesses have been reporting for more than one hundred years:

> The nocturnal light glows in the distance or moves up the road toward you as fast as a person could walk. At closer ranges, people have seen it as round, spherical or diamond-shaped, the

size of a lantern light or large as a washtub. You can see trees and bushes through it, says one observer. It may float past you, dance around or split and shoot off in different directions. This itinerant mystery is in the road, in a field, in the woods, at the window of a house. It's golden or red, or it appears as multiple lights in various combinations of yellow, orange, red, green and blue.

I have found accounts in which people described minor injuries to themselves or their vehicles when they became "spooked" and were too hasty in trying to get away, but I have found no reports of the Spook Light doing anyone bodily harm. One woman said she thought the light had caused a small burn mark on the paint job of the family car. Several said the light seemed to pass right through them with no obvious effect.

You can find residents who swear they must have seen the lights by now hundreds of times, and other locals who have never seen them yet. The lights used to be seen most commonly near County Road E 40, on the Missouri side, but in the 1950s folks say the lights seemed to move south, closer to E 50 just over the line in Oklahoma. Depending on who you ask, you will get advice to park in Missouri and look toward Oklahoma, or, no, do it just the other way around. Some sightings of the lights appeared to witnesses to be right alongside automobiles parked some distance away, but when the individuals in those seemingly nearby cars were asked, they said they saw nothing (cue the *Twilight Zone* theme).

Recently "No Parking" signs were posted on the Ottawa County (Oklahoma) side of the border on E 50, which locals call Spook Light Road. A call to the sheriff's department elicited a reply that parking should be limited to five minutes. I do not know how long it will take some enterprising individual to discover that providing safe parking, a shuttle service, and a place to get warm, or cool, or dry, might just be a money maker. But that would spoil the scary fun of just driving out, late at night, wandering around a little, asking other earth light hunters in hushed tones:

"Have you seen it?"

"No, you?"

"No, but I came out with some of my friends last week, and it was over there . . ."

Sometimes, especially around Halloween, you might see or be interviewed by a local television news crew. National networks have filmed specials on the Spook Light. Groups of area residents have formed their own investigative clubs that you might encounter there, too. This is a mystery that attracts psychics and physicists, grandparents and their grandchildren. Something exists that has been drawing people for uncounted years. Like sitting around, watching a campfire, or staring at the ocean waves roll in, the activity is mesmerizing and magical. Something in the origin of earth lights fascinates us and causes one's mind to contemplate unknowable things. Most people who return to see the lights often will tell you Earth does have a spirit, and earth lights are a means by which she is trying to communicate with us. If we could only understand, and if others would just listen.

BIBLIOGRAPHY

CHAPTER 1: JIM THE WONDER DOG

Cadoret, Remi. "Chris the Wonder Dog." *Journal of Parapsychology*, March 1958.

Counts, Evelyn. "Jim's Story." www.jimthewonderdog.com. Accessed June 6, 2012.

Fatheree, Kay Murphy. "Kemmerer's Anniversary of Jim the Wonder Dog." *Kemmerer Gazette*, September 2, 2010.

Ferguson, Henry. "Jim the Wonderdog." *Rural Missouri*, April, 1979.

Offutt, Jason. From-the-shadows.blogspot.com/2007/03/jim-wonder-dog.html. Accessed June 6, 2012.

CHAPTER 2: TEMPUS FUGIT WHILE A CAVE KEEPS ITS SECRETS

Conrad, Howard Louis. *Encyclopedia of the History of Missouri*. New York: Southern History Company, 1901.

Cozad, Mary. Neosho: *The Story of a Missouri Town, A Short History*. Safeway Stores, 1965.

James, Larry A. Neosho, *The First Century 1839–1939*. Neosho, MO: The Neosho County Historical Society, 2001.

Meeker, Scott. "Newton County Official Thinks He's Found Lost Civil War Cave." *Joplin Globe*. Reprinted in the *Southeast Missourian*, April 6, 2002.

CHAPTER 3: THIS MISSOURI HIDEOUT WAS NOT A JESSE JAMES CAVE

The Beatles. *The Beatles Anthology*. San Francisco: Chronicle Books, 2002.

http://meetthebeatlesforreal.blogspot.com/2010/05/beatles-slept-here.html. Accessed August 8, 2013.

www.beatlesbible.com/diary.com. Accessed August 8, 2013.

CHAPTER 4: THE LOST SILVER MINE AND THE MYSTERY OF YOCUM DOLLARS

Ayres, Artie. *Traces of Silver*. Reeds Spring, MO: The Ozark Mountain Historical Society, 1982.

Morrow, Lynn. "The Yocum Silver Dollar." *White River Valley Historical Quarterly*, Volume 8, Number 11, Spring 1985.

Schoolcraft, Henry. *Scenes and Adventures in the Semi-Alpine Region of the Ozark Mountains of Missouri and Arkansas*. Philadelphia: Lippincott, Grambo & Co., 1853.

CHAPTER 5: A LARGER-THAN-LIFE LADY

Chasteen, Barbara. *Ella K. Ewing, Missouri Giantess: 1872–1913*. Memphis, MO: Scotland Public Library, 1977.

http://memphisdemocrat.com/2013/news/130110_missella
.shtml. Date accessed August 7, 2013.

McEowen, Bob. "A Towering Spirit." *Rural Missouri*, March
2003.

Memphis Democrat. "Legend of Miss Ella Still Stands Tall 100
Years After Her Passing." January 10, 2013.

Wiley, Bette J. *Our Miss Ella*. Memphis, MO: Bette J. Wiley,
1995.

CHAPTER 6: IN NEW MADRID ORDER THE MALT, NOT A SHAKE
Audubon, J. J. *Audubon and His Journals*. New York: Scribner,
1897.

"Eyewitnesses to Mississippi River earthquake terror." www.
Showme.net/~fkeller/quake/lib/eyewitness1.htm. Accessed
August 10, 2013.

Johnston, Arch C., and Eugene S. Schweig. "The Enigma of the
New Madrid Earthquakes of 1811–1812." *Annual Review of
Earth and Planetary Sciences*, 1996.

Latrobe, John H. B. *The First Steamboat Voyage on the Western
Waters*. Baltimore: Maryland Historical Society, 1871.

Rural Arkansas Living. "New Madrid Earthquakes' Bicentennial
Puts Focus on Preparedness." March 2011.

CHAPTER 7: TOM BASS: LEGENDARY HORSE WHISPERER

O'Reilly, CuChullaine. "Whisper on the Wind: The Tom Bass Story." *Horse Connection* magazine, November 2008.

Tom Bass Memorial Edition (a collection of newspaper articles from throughout his life). Mexico, MO: *The Mexico Evening Ledger*, 1949. Reprinted 1991.

CHAPTER 8: MASTODONS AND MAMMOTHS IN MISSOURI

"Information Release." Mastodon State Historic Site, 2010.

Waters, Michael R., et al. "Pre-Clovis Mastodon Hunting 13,800 Years Ago at the Manis Site, Washington." *Science*, October 2011.

Zimmer, Carl. "Bringing Them Back to Life." *National Geographic*, April 2013.

CHAPTER 9: THE THREE SPRINGFIELD WOMEN: VANISHED

Baird, Kathee. "Nineteen Years Later . . . Sherrill, Suzie and Stacy Are Still Missing." Crimesceneinvestigations.blogspot .com/2011/06/nineteen-year. Accessed August 23, 2013.

Springfield Police Department. www.springfieldmo.gov/spd/ generalinfo/3missingwomen.html. Accessed August 23, 2013.

Streeterfamilyblogg.blogspot.com. Accessed August 23, 2013.

CHAPTER 10: THE FLIGHT OF THE *ATLANTIC*: FUELED BY PLENTY OF HOT AIR

Moehlmann, Nick. "John Wise, A Pioneer." *The John Wise Balloon Society Newsletter*. www.johnwise.net/jw.html. Accessed September 1, 2013.

Naughton, Russell. *The Pioneers, John Wise*. Victoria, Australia: Monash University Engineering Department, 2007.

The Union. "Interesting Adventures Above Lake Ontario." July 13, 1859.

CHAPTER 11: SEARCHING FOR ROUND ROCKS AND STARDUST

Beauford, Robert. "Ancient Meteorite Impact Craters of the Ozark Plateau." *The Ozarks Mountaineer*, May/June 2012.

Chiles, James R. "Weaubleaus Round Rocks." Disaster-wise .blogspot.com/2011/12/weaubleaus-round-rocks-html. Accessed September 5, 2013.

Ernstson, Kord, and Ferran Claudin. "The Weaubleau impact structure 'round rocks.'" www.impact-structures .com/2013/07. Accessed September 5, 2013.

Penprase, Mike. "Evidence of meteorite found near Osceola." *Springfield News Leader*, April 12, 2003.

Smith, Stephen. "The Weaubleau-Osceola Structure." www .thunderbolts.info 2009. Accessed September 5, 2013.

CHAPTER 12: JESSE JAMES LIVES ON IN INFAMY

Settle, William A. *Jesse James Was His Name*. Lincoln: University of Nebraska Press, 1977.

Slotkin, Richard. *Gunfighter Nation: The Myth of the Frontier in Twentieth-Century America*. Norman, OK: University of Oklahoma Press, 1998.

Stiles, T. J. *Jesse James: Last Rebel of the Civil War*. New York: Knopf, 2002.

CHAPTER 13: EARTH LIGHT, EARTH BRIGHT, HOPE I SEE A LIGHT TONIGHT

Adams, Marsha, et al. www.earthlights.org. Accessed September 9, 2013.

Kaczmarek, Dale. "Joplin Spooklight Investigation." www.ghostresearch.org/Investigations/Joplin.html 2004. Accessed September 9, 2013.

Palmer, Sean B. "The Hornet Spooklight." inamidst.com/lights/hornet. Accessed September 9, 2013.

Wilson, Suzanne. "Spooklight." *Missouri Conservationist*, January 1997.

INDEX

ABOUT THE AUTHOR

Josh Young transited Missouri countless times before he ever thought he wanted to live in the Show Me State. A graduate of the University of New Hampshire and Indiana University, Josh taught kids from college to kindergarten before doing a stint as a family services caseworker. One year, when he should have known better, he shouldered a sixty-pound backpack, hitchhiking around the United States. That grand adventure introduced him to the Missouri/Arkansas Ozarks.

Settling on a little farm deep in the woods near Branson (with Johnny and June Cash for neighbors briefly), Josh continued social work, while garnering a few awards for a locally syndicated humor column. He currently works and plays at his home on Long Creek Herb Farm. He is still trying to decide what to do when he grows up.